THE
GAP-YEAR
ADVANTAGE

THE
GAP-YEAR
ADVANTAGE

Helping Your Child
Benefit from Time Off
Before or During College

KARL HAIGLER
and
RAE NELSON

 ST. MARTIN'S GRIFFIN 🦅 NEW YORK

www.stmartins.com

Library of Congress Cataloging-in-Publication Data

Haigler, Karl.
The gap-year advantage: helping your child benefit from time off before or during college /
Karl Haigler and Rae Nelson.—1st St. Martin's Griffin ed.
p. cm.
ISBN 0-312-33698-5
EAN 978-0-312-33698-1
1. Gap years. 2. Non-formal education. 3. Experiential learning. I. Nelson, Rae. II. Title.
LC45.3.H35 2005
378.1'98—dc22
2004028864

First Edition: August 2005

10 9 8 7 6 5 4 3 2 1

To
Cornelius H. Bull.
A man of great heart, humor, and vision who
helped us see the risks of the ordinary.

Contents

PART 1

PART 2: Programs and Resources

I. Programs

II. Resources

PART 1

Introduction: Intrepid Pathways

"I'M NOT SURE I want to go to college next year."

This was the first indication we had that our eighteen-year-old son, Adam, although accepted by selective colleges, was considering stepping off the traditional road of education to journey down a path less traveled.

"But I do have an idea of what I want to do!" he continued. Adam was inspired by a graduate of a school in his district who had taken time off before college to participate in a community service program called City Year. The young man, Matt Hendren, had returned to his alma mater and dropped by Adam's government and politics class to talk about his experiences.

"I was about to enroll in an excellent but very large university," Matt Hendren reported. "I didn't have the focus or exposure to seek out what I wanted to do. If you have any doubt that you will succeed, take time off to *ensure* you will succeed. For

me, City Year was the perfect mix of teaching, learning, exposure to the real world, and responsibility. Taking time off and
serving through City Year was the best decision of my life."
Matt's description of teaching fourth-graders in a rooftop garden in Boston, Massachusetts, sparked an interest in Adam that
was more relevant and focused than his vision of spending at
least four more years sitting in classrooms.

While Adam spoke convincingly about how taking time off
might be the right option for him, we recalled a time not too
long ago when some in our generation had acted on President
Kennedy's assertion that "one person can make a difference
and every person should try" through the Peace Corps or Volunteers In Service to America (VISTA). And many more of
us—at least those not called by military service—had heard the
words but continued unquestioningly and dutifully down the
road prescribed by our schools, our parents, and our society.
We also recalled conversations with a few peers who chose to
set forth in the 1960s, 1970s, and 1980s on gap-year opportunities before or during college. They—like Adam's City Year
schoolmate—considered the experience powerful, pivotal, and
life changing.

As Adam wondered about the options that might be
open to him if he took time off, Karl recalled how, more than
twenty years earlier, as a principal of Heathwood Hall in
South Carolina, several of his students had questioned whether
they were ready for college . . . yet. At that time, he had a for-
tuitous encounter with Cornelius "Neil" Bull, an educator and
visionary, who made the case that there were alternatives to
going straight to college for students who were prepared to
choose them.

Inspired by Adam's interest, we made a quick search of the
Internet. We found that Neil Bull's vision had grown into the

Center for Interim Programs, LLC, located in Princeton, New Jersey, and Cambridge, Massachusetts. Interim is a locus for helping thousands of students design and implement customized gap-year strategies. Soon Adam was on a conference call with Holly Bull, Neil's daughter and the Center's interim president. She described the myriad opportunities open to him if he was interested in pursuing intrepid pathways.

As we grew accustomed to the prospect of Adam's stepping off the beaten track to college, we were reassured by the examples of other families who had been the beneficiaries of the Interim experience. Holly (like her father before her) ensured our involvement every step along the way, delving into our view of Adam's options—and particularly reinforcing his college goals as an integral part of an overall plan. By the time of our initial phone interview with Holly, we believed Adam was prepared, along with us, to consider the prospects of taking time off as part of his educational and (perhaps) life goals.

"Would you like to work with a group in Central America? Explore where *The Lord of the Rings* trilogy was filmed in New Zealand? Volunteer as a forest ranger in the Redwoods? Teach environmental studies in Appalachia? Intern with the British parliament?" Adam's eyes grew wide as Holly was able to connect with exactly what Adam was hoping for: These were *his* options! He *did* have choices!

What emerged from these conference calls—and the conversations we had with Adam around them—was a plan for an "extra-curriculum" sequence of events that, combined, would last a year or more. Adam's gap experiences would begin with a weeklong outdoor education program in New Jersey at Tom Brown, Jr.'s Tracker School and then would take him overseas to teach in Costa Rica and to work on an environmental preserve in New Zealand, finally leading him to a job in Texas as an instructor in environmental education. Holly's sense of Adam's goals provided a rationale for each program he considered and its respective place in the overall plan.

The first stage in Adam's international journey was ten weeks living with a host family in a small mountain village in Costa Rica and teaching English with another volunteer in the local elementary school through a program called Global Routes. The growth, maturity, and perspective that he gained were evident to us in numerous ways, but can be illustrated through e-mails written at that time. He discovered through working with kids who were incredibly excited about learning that teaching was his calling. His fluency in Spanish grew exponentially as he became immersed in the life of the village.

He also gained a perspective on the value of resources. "In my school there is absolutely nothing," he wrote in one e-mail. He proposed to develop a fund for textbooks and scholarships. "Tons of the kids here want to go to school but can't go past sixth grade because of the lack of funds," he relayed. "Their hunger for learning and teaching in Costa Rica is awesome and has totally changed my view on education." During his time in Central America, he managed to raise more than two thousand dollars for books and scholarships, mostly through contacts at his former high school.

Last Thanksgiving, he sent this e-mail to his family: "It's amazing that this part of my life is about to end. It seems like a few days ago that I arrived in San José, and now I'm five days away from leaving. This experience has been the best thing that ever happened to me, and I appreciate all the support you all gave me throughout. My village will be forever thankful to you guys, and you can know that you really have made friends in Costa Rica."

The e-mails and the stories he has shared since provide only a hint of the breadth and depth of Adam's experiences and the strength of the bonds he developed with his host family, his students, and his peers in the Global Routes program.

Adam's experiences were eye-opening to us, as parents, and we continue to be amazed and inspired by Adam's growth, development, and contributions during and after his time-off experiences. As Adam learned, so did we.

With a combined forty years of experience in public policy, we have been able to contribute to debates and initiatives regarding what can be done to improve educational outcomes for students. As teachers and parents, we've had the opportunity to help guide students in their options regarding post–high school choices. But, as effective educators will confide, the right personal stories can be extremely instructive. And we've rarely encountered stories as powerful as those of students who've taken time off before or during college. They have been able to learn more about themselves, and, at an age when many still call them kids, they have given back to the world in ways many adults could not even imagine.

This book is based on the stories of the dozens of students we've met and interviewed who've chosen to follow their own intrepid paths. It also is based on the experiences of dozens more families, counselors, program leaders, teachers, and other educators who have supported them along the way. The examples and practical advice in these pages are offered in the hope that many other young Americans and their families will step off the traditional road and benefit from the gap-year advantage—and come to believe, as we do, that we can all gain a better perspective on our place in the world and the wisdom that will help us in our journey through it.

We look forward to hearing more stories and learning of your journeys in the months and years ahead.

Karl Haigler and Rae Nelson
Advance, North Carolina
2005

1

Reality Check

You have to do your own growing no matter how tall your grandfather was.

—ABRAHAM LINCOLN

THE STAKES ARE HIGH for the almost fifteen million high school students who will return to classrooms this fall, most with the goal of attending a college or university immediately after graduation. Armed with guides, marketing brochures, and Web site information, parents will diligently do what they can to see that their child's class rank is advanced, SAT and ACT scores are maximized, and extracurricular activities are amassed—whatever it takes to ensure that their child is accepted into the right college.

Come spring, acceptance letters will be received at homes across the country as students and parents wait—anxiously, expectantly—to see which colleges have said yes.

Congratulations! The chances are good that your child has gotten into at least one school. The more than two thousand days he or she has spent in classrooms, and the time, energy, and resources you have devoted to the application process have paid off. Many parents will breathe a sigh of relief. Their child has been accepted at college! And now he or she is one step closer to realizing their part of the American Dream.

Five years from now, however, many students and their parents may wish they had focused as much on having *success* in college as they had on gaining *access* to college.

According to the American College Testing service, less than half of those entering traditional four-year colleges after high school will have graduated after five years. One-quarter will have dropped out during their freshman year. Of those in college, many will report that they do not know why they are there or how their classes relate to any life or career goal. Many of those in school, as well as those who have left, will have accumulated considerable debt without a realistic chance of finding a job that matches their educational level.

For a number of these students, a gap-year plan may make the difference between graduating successfully from college with a strategy for life beyond and floating uncertainly on a path of young adulthood that may be accompanied by significant financial and emotional costs. Through the gap year, for the first time in their highly structured lives, students may have the opportunity to discover and follow their passion and to truly live in the present.

The benefits of a gap-year plan include gaining confidence, focus, and discipline, being able to bridge the gap between formal education and the real world, and building a résumé that will put students ahead of their peers in appealing to employers or graduate schools. In addition, students (and their parents!) with a gap-year plan may save thousands of dollars in college tuition, student loans, and scholarships. Less tangible, but perhaps most important, gap-year students will have the experience of taking responsibility for their lives and thereby gaining greater perspective on their place in the world and how they may uniquely contribute to their communities and families now and in the future.

A gap-year plan is not for every student, but it may make sense for your child or another young person you know. In this book, you will meet students who have incorporated such a plan into their college strategy. You will also meet their parents and others who have provided support, wisdom, and counsel. These supporters, as you will see, have even learned more about themselves along the way.

You've met Adam. He was in the top 20 percent of his class in high school and a natural comedian who excelled at sports. He was determined to see the world beyond his community and get a sense of his place in it before going to college. His gap-year experiences so far have included attending Tracker School in the wilds of New Jersey, teaching in Costa Rica, working on an environmental conservation trust in New Zealand, and teaching environmental studies to inner-city youth in Texas. In addition to describing this time as the "best experience of my life," he now will apply to colleges that more closely match the growing interests he's nurtured in education, the environment, and service during his gap year.

Rusty Whatley's planning for a gap year began in the summer before his senior year. Due to some health problems during his high school years in Birmingham, Alabama, Rusty and his parents agreed that he could use the time off before college to gain strength as well as experience in vigorous outdoor activities.

From the list of options developed through consulting with the Center for Interim Programs, Rusty and his parents settled on two programs: in the first semester after high school graduation, he worked as a cabin steward aboard the *Mystic Whaler,* a vintage sailing ship that provides educational and recreational cruises on major rivers and ports in the Northeast; during the second semester, he worked as a field hand on a polo ranch in Hawaii, performing daily chores such as building fences and pitching hay.

A critical part of this planning was Rusty's gaining a deferral of admission to the University of Alabama, his college of choice. Rusty was responsible for submitting this request letter, the central point of which was his explanation of what he would be doing during his year off.

Among the goals that Rusty and his parents set for the year, that of his gaining physical strength was a clear benefit. Other unanticipated outcomes included his falling in love with ocean sailing, gaining an increased respect for what it means to work with one's hands, and his becoming more aware of why he wanted to go to college. Today, Rusty is enrolled at the University of Alabama and doing well.

Joseph George Demille grew up in South Boston and dropped out of school at the age of sixteen to work odd jobs in order to support his mother, brothers, and himself. He discovered opportunities for community service through a friend who was participating in City Year in Boston. Among his responsibilities with City Year was leading a service day, during which he instructed and managed people in revitalizing a gym in Roslindale, Massachusetts, outside of Boston. His obvious leadership abilities caught the eye of a *Boston Globe* reporter, and Joe was featured on the front page of the Sunday Living Arts section of the newspaper. A few weeks later, Boston College officials offered him a full four-year scholarship. Joe worked two jobs that summer—at the Department of Youth Services in Boston and at the local AIDS Action Committee—before starting school.

Erika Dickson was a sophomore at the University of Michigan when she came to see that she was burned out. She told her parents that she should stop wasting their money because she didn't even know what to major in yet. Instead of leaving school, Erika drew on her school's encouragement to go abroad and did research on the Internet. She took a semester off to travel to Ghana. There she lived with a host family in a small village and taught English. "The experience changed my life," Erika recalls. She credits the experience with her deciding to major in premed. She plans to return to Ghana and "do a lot of work in Africa."

These stories—as well as the statistics on college dropout rates—should lead you as a parent of a student considering post–high school options to step back early in the college application process and ask yourself a few questions:

- Have you asked your child *why* she wants to go to college after high school (instead of *where* does she want to go to school)?
- Are you focused on ensuring your child has *access* to the right college—or on her *success* in college and life beyond?
- Is your child—your eighteen-, nineteen-, or twenty-year-old—ready to succeed in college now?
- Does your child have not only the academic preparation, but also the focus, discipline, and maturity to take full advantage of perhaps the most pivotal transition period in her young life?

If you hesitated before answering these questions, it may be time for a reality check.

NOT THE SAME OL' COLLEGE GAME

Like many parents of high school students today, you probably are familiar with how the college application game was played in the 1960s, 1970s, or 1980s. Even if you didn't attend a post–secondary institution yourself, you are likely to be familiar with someone who did. The fact is that the college game has changed significantly over the past three decades.

Let's take a snapshot of the 1970s as a case in point and, in particular, consider three trends—students, finances, and graduation rates.

In the good ol' days, there was roughly the same number of baby boomers as there are teenagers today. In 1974, there were about fifteen million students in high school (grades nine through twelve) and about half of them went directly to college after graduation. The majority of those attending post–secondary institutions were "traditional" students—that is, they were in their late teens or early twenties, were enrolled full-time, and worked little or not at all. Almost half of these college students received a degree within four years. At a price: The class of 1974 accumulated approximately $90 million in student loans. Even though there may have been gas lines and high interest rates, college graduates who were persistent found jobs—jobs that matched their educational level and interest.

Fast-forward thirty years to today. There is little doubt that a college education is more valuable today than ever. The National Commission on the High School Senior Year (developed through a partnership among the U.S. Department of Education, the Carnegie Corporation, the Charles Stewart Mott Foundation, and the Woodrow Wilson National Fellowship Foundation to study the value of the last year of secondary school) states the issue bluntly: "In the agricultural age, post–secondary education was a pipe dream for most Americans. In the industrial age, it was the birthright of only a few. By the space age, it became common sense for many. Today, it is just common sense for all."

One reason many assert that higher education makes sense as a goal for most students is dollars. For example, it has been documented that there is an income gap of more than $50,000 per year between a high school dropout and a holder of a college degree—and it lasts a lifetime.

TIME OUT OR BURN OUT

A significant difference for today's students is the intense pressure to be accepted by the "right college" and the related threats of anxiety, stress, and "burning out." Studies reported by the American Psychological Association's *Journal of Personality and Social Psychology* (December 2002), for example, reveal that average schoolkids in recent decades report more anxiety than child psychiatric patients did during the 1950s.

Harvard College officials summarized the impact of the pressure on the current generation in a widely noted essay released in 2002. In "Time Out or Burn Out for the Next Generation," William Fitzsimmons, dean of admissions and financial aid; Marlyn McGrath Lewis, director of admissions; and Charles Ducey, director of the bureau of study counsel—all at Harvard—argue that students who are on the treadmill of getting into the right schools (sometimes starting before kindergarten) and the right colleges, under pressure to find the right jobs and drive the right car through the right neighborhood, risk emerging as "dazed survivors of some bewildering lifelong boot camp." They become adults who, looking back from the fast track, have "missed their youth entirely, never living in the present, always pursuing some ill-defined future goal." The writers conclude, from their unique perspective as college admissions officers: "Let us hope that more of them take time out before burn out becomes the hallmark of their generation."

Harvard administrators aren't the only ones who are aware that many students aren't ready for college.

Hal Shear's unique perspective stems from his work with the federal government in running Job Corps and Neighborhood Youth Corps programs. His daughter, Anya, took time off before college, a decision he supported. It confirmed his notion that the ages of eighteen through twenty are especially crucial for students who need to gain a sense of responsibility. Gap-year programs, both privately and publicly sponsored, he says, can be of immense value in getting young people over the hump and starting them off on the right foot. Anya's increased sense of personal responsibility during the year she spent working as an assistant in a high-tech firm contributed to her graduating in four years from the University of Massachusetts at Amherst.

The undercurrent of concern over students' readiness for higher education is reflected on Web sites where current and former college officials, who may be reluctant to voice their opinions formally, exchange messages.

"I was a physics professor and taught many freshmen, including premeds. Many of these students simply were not ready for college. They lacked the maturity, skills, and so on, and quite a few, particularly the premeds, were there by virtue of parental pressure. In fact, the problems of these unfortunate students were of concern to all faculty members." So reads one entry on an Internet message board. The entry concludes, "On the other hand, many students who had worked or done special studies for a couple of years after high school did brilliantly—they were studying because they wanted to do so."

THE PRESSURE IS ON

With the pressure on, most high school students today report they plan to attend college or university following graduation. Indeed, more than 60 percent of them will achieve the goal of entering college (up from about 50 percent in 1974). Once on campus, however, the student profile differs from what the parents may remember. Less than 20 percent of the students in a college or university today (including community colleges) are traditional.

One reason the college application game has changed is that, in spite of increased competition to get into the most selective schools, *access* to college isn't much of a problem today. There are currently more than 4,000 post–secondary institutions (30 percent more than in 1974), most of which would love to have your child on their campus—accompanied, of course, by tuition and probably room and board fees. The average institution of higher learning accepts more than 70 percent of those that apply. In other words, if your child wants to get into a college or a university, the chances are that he or she will.

Have you noticed that there is more marketing material arriving at your door from colleges than you remember thirty years ago? Competition for your child—and the money flow that follows him—is growing. According to a survey conducted by the National Association of College Admission Counseling, 70 percent of post–secondary institutions have undergone a public relations overhaul to make themselves more attractive to potential students.

High school counselors are professionals dedicated to help-ing you and your child sort through the maze of post–secondary options. However, in public schools, the ratio of students to counselors is 490 to 1 on average. (It's better in private schools.) These experts, to put it mildly, are stretched thin.

For additional assistance in the application process, some parents turn to the private sector. College consultants can charge thousands of dollars for advice on issues such as choosing the right school, nailing the interview, or writing the perfect admissions essay. There also is growing business in preparation classes for the SAT and ACT exams and sales of college guides and related merchandise. There are even getting-into-college camps that, for almost $3,000, will take students through twelve days of test prep, applications strategies, and college visits.

For those who are accepted by a college and have financial barriers, money generally is available for those willing to sign on the dotted line. Federal student loans have jumped more than 300 percent since 1974. Just between 1990 and 2000, federal student lending doubled from $16.4 billion to $37.5 billion. The number of loans allocated each year during the same time frame rose from 4.5 million to 9.4 million—more than double! In addition, there is a growing trend toward private student lending options. According to the College Board (a nonprofit organization perhaps best known for its SAT pro-gram) students borrowed almost $4 billion in 2000–2001 from private lending institutions (compared to $1.5 billion in 1995–1996).

It may be an understatement to say that higher education is big business in America today.

Let's go back to your child who is planning to become one

of the more than eight million students enrolled at a four-year college or university in the United States in the near future. And let's say that he or she is accepted and decides to attend the fall after high school graduation. As noted earlier in this chapter, less than half of those entering college will have earned a degree within five years.

It's safe to say that for many of today's high school students (and their parents), the concept of college success—defined by graduating with a degree in four years—could turn into a more circuitous path that may be accompanied by significant financial and emotional challenges.

The bottom line is that applying to college is becoming an increasingly stressful, complex, and expensive process that focuses primarily on admission as the endgame. The reality is that *success* in college today—as in work and life—is not solely the responsibility of an institution or government. It is the responsibility of the student, ideally with the support of the parents and other committed adults.

As a committed parent, guardian, or other adult caring for a high school student, what can you do to help your child?

The first step is to recognize that you are uniquely positioned to support and guide your student when it comes to such an important decision as to where and *when* to go to college. In fact, surveys report that most teenagers believe that helping them take school seriously is one of the most valuable roles parents can play in their lives.

In this book you'll meet a number of students—and their parents—who have benefited from the gap-year advantage. You will learn the details and keys to structuring a plan that makes sense for your child's interests, talents, and potential.

It is worth reiterating that attending college is a valuable goal for most students. But it may not be the right course for your child *right now*! Taking time off may not make sense for all students. But it just might provide a foundation of wisdom, experience, responsibility, and perspective that will help your child to get the most out of college—and life beyond.

2

The Gap-Year Tradition

Let us unleash the power of young people in all nations to see the world for what it is now, and then go out to change it for the better.
—SARGENT SHRIVER, FOUNDING DIRECTOR OF THE PEACE CORPS

THE TRADITION OF TAKING "time off with a purpose"—whether to renew one's spirit, explore new worlds, gain perspective, fulfill an obligation, learn a new skill, or reconnect with a passion for learning—is centuries old. It is deeply embedded in many cultures, in mythic tales, heraldic legends, and classic literature that revolve around young adventurers setting out on quests that lead, in part, to greater self-discovery. *The Pilgrim's Progress, Gulliver's Travels,* and *Siddhartha* are examples.

In Australia, the "walkabout" stems from an Aboriginal tradition, and Germans can enjoy a *Wanderjahr* (or a year of wandering). A number of religions, such as the Mormons, prescribe missions for college-aged youth. Many parents and grandparents of today's students participated in a government-sponsored version of the gap-year advantage—through military or alternative service.

For centuries indigenous cultures, such as the Native Americans, have centered on the vision quest as a way for members of a tribe to discover which direction to take in life or to seek an answer to a profound question. (A vision quest usually involves a period of isolation that leads to internal reflection, revelation, and transformation.)

The British gap year is, perhaps, what many Americans are most familiar with when it comes to describing students' taking a break before college. The number of "gappers" in the United Kingdom is reported to be growing at a rate of 15 percent a year. Some attribute the growth in participants to Prince William and Prince Harry, whose gap-year experiences were widely chronicled in the global press. In Britain, the vast majority of college admissions officers and employers are in favor of gap-year experiences and the Department of Education and Skills (similar to our federal Department of Education) endorses them.

In the United States, however, taking time off or a gap-year option is a relatively new concept, though the spirit of exploration is certainly central to our national character. Pioneers, explorers, and adventurers have heeded the call to "Go West, young man!" since before the birth of our nation. In the 1860s, Mark Twain captured the popular trend of Americans' journeying to "the Continent" in his landmark work *The Innocents Abroad.* "I basked in the happiness of being for once in my life drifting with the tide of a great popular movement. Everybody was going to Europe," he wrote.

Nearly a century later (in the 1960s and 1970s), fortunate students in the United States were treated to a summer of European travel after high school. Others backpacked through France and Germany, leveraging Eurail passes and staying in youth hostels along the way.

The organized time-off tradition in America of the last twenty years is most often attributed to Cornelius (Neil) Bull, a pioneer and visionary who was dedicated to inspiring students and other individuals to explore time-off options and guiding them through the process of planning and implementing an American version of the gap experience. As headmaster of Verde Valley School in Sedona, Arizona, in the late 1960s, he witnessed the impact of service experience and cultural immersion on his students when they worked on Navajo reservations and in towns in Mexico as part of their curriculum. Impressed by the positive impact this experience made in the lives of his students, he became a powerful advocate for similar options. Neil's advocacy for students taking time off caught the attention of media and opinion makers as well as students and parents, leading to the establishment of the Center for Interim Programs, LLC, located in Princeton, New Jersey, and Cambridge, Massachusetts.

Over the past twenty-five years, thousands of individuals have been guided by Neil's vision and hands-on, personalized approach. They credit him with being ahead of his time in thinking about alternatives to traditional education. Today, leadership has been passed to Neil's daughter, Holly Bull, who heads Interim and carries on the tradition of providing options, structure, and support to students and their families before and during their gap-year journeys.

There is no concrete research showing how many students are American "gappers" today, but it's safe to say that at least tens of thousands take time off before or during college. It may be called "deferring college," "an interim year," or simply "taking a break." This book is designed for those students and their families who may be interested in becoming a part of these collective experiences that add up to the gap-year advantage.

What is the Gap-Year Advantage?

The gap-year advantage stems from taking time off before or during college to participate in a structured set of experiences that may include community service, volunteering, interning, work, study, travel, or any combination of these. The total amount of time off may last from a semester up to two years, but many students choose to spend a year on this unique path to self-exploration. Individual segments may last from as short as a week-long break in between formal programs to a year-long commitment. The gap-year plan includes building in time to process and reflect on experiences and to address college application strategies. A family may work with a consultant who will guide them through time-off options, or the student may set specific goals, follow passions, design an individualized set of experiences, or participate in programs such as those described in part 2 of this book.

Young Americans today have a number of diverse choices among gap-year or time-off plans, with the ability to customize a sequence of experiences regardless of their income or background. Most students describe their time off as life-changing experiences, and they would recommend that others consider it as a part of the transition to maturity as well as a part of planning for college.

What is the Difference Between a Gap-Year Plan
and Just "Goofing Off" Before or During College?

The motivation for either of these options may, initially, be the same. Students who have been on the fast track, who are burned out amassing credentials on the way to college, or who just want to explore the world may need a break before plunging into a multiyear commitment to the academic grind.

Without a plan, a structure, and goals, some young people may yield to the temptation to just hang out, travel with friends, or bum around. Days can turn into weeks, the seasons will change, and then a year or more has passed, and these young people may be no more focused than when they left high school. The process of seriously thinking through time-off options and coming up with a plan can help develop even the most fledgling notions of what might be accomplished during a break. With a flexible structure, a time-off experience can become meaningful and purposeful. The journey can also become more developmental when a student joins with others in exploring different lands and cultures or participating in service opportunities that engage not only a young adult's curiosity but also encourage personal growth. A gap-year plan, then, is founded on a social *and* solitary pursuit of real-world experience as a mode of learning and growth.

Gap-Year Terms

GAP YEAR. A gap year is a period of time a student takes as a break from formal education to travel, volunteer, study, or work. A gap experience generally ranges from one semester up to two years and frequently is taken between high school and college but may be taken during college. Also referred to as "time off" or "interim."

HOMESTAY. A homestay is when a student participating in a gap-year program or experience away from home (e.g., in another country) lives with a family in the host country. The homestay experience generally is designed to foster strong relationships and intercultural understanding among the student and host family members.

HOST FAMILY. A student may live with a host family when participating in a program that involves an extended period of time away from home (e.g., a homestay in another state or foreign country). A host family provides a home, food, encouragement, support, and generally treats a student as a member of the family during a gap-year experience.

IMMERSION EXPERIENCE. Immersion describes a program in which a student is engaged wholly in the topic he or she is interested in and placed in surroundings that support the goal of immersion. For example, a student in a language immersion program may live in a foreign country and be requested to speak only in the foreign language; a student in a cultural immersion program may live with a family in another country.

INTERNSHIP. An internship provides a student with practical, hands-on experience at a place of work under the supervision of an organization's employee. Interns may be paid or may not be paid. Internships provide students with insight into the world of work and may help students explore various careers.

SERVICE LEARNING. Service learning is a method through which students grow through participating in meaningful, structured activities designed to address community needs. Service learning frequently combines community service with formal academic instruction.

STUDY ABROAD. The term study abroad refers to students' participating in educational activities outside the United States. Study abroad generally refers to formal academic programs but may include internships and service learning experiences.

Why do Students Take a Gap Year?

The reasons for taking a gap year are as varied as the students who take them. Many report simply being burned out after competing on a high-pressure playing field from elementary grades through high school. Some students want to serve or contribute to a cause bigger than themselves (and not wait four or more years to make a difference). Others want to try to answer the question "Why should I go to college . . . now?" (beyond the proverbial "Because you are expected to" that comes from many parents, counselors, and well-meaning adults). Some have a specific goal they want to reach or a passion that they wish to pursue. A number of students hear about the idea from a friend or colleague and it simply resonates. There are other cases where a parent or a teacher introduces the option to students.

For every student who takes time off, there are many others who consider the option and choose not to pursue it. The most frequently cited reason that a young American wouldn't choose to take a break? Parents.

"I know kids who thought about it, but were afraid their parents would say no without giving the idea a fair chance," stated one veteran gapper who reflected the sentiments of other students we interviewed. "Other parents didn't think their children were responsible enough to handle it. But if you trust your kids, you should let them follow a dream. You have no idea how they'll grow and how much they'll thank you in the end."

What Can You Do During Time Off?

We've categorized the types of experiences that a student can participate in as community service and volunteering, studying, interning and working, and exploring and traveling. Within these four categories, the programs and specific experiences can be as varied as you can imagine or design. Students we profiled studied at Oxford, hiked the Appalachian Trail, watched whales in Maui, worked on environmental preserves in New Zealand, taught English in Costa Rica and Ghana, trekked in Thailand, taught environmental studies on the rooftops of Boston, studied the impact of elk in national parks, turned a passion for skateboarding into a business opportunity, interned with sports teams, and had many other varied experiences.

Most participated in a series of activities within a six-month to two-year period taking time in between to process experiences, work to save money, or apply to colleges.

Chapter 4 in this book breaks down the options in greater detail and part 2 includes information on programs and resources that provide just a taste of the thousands of opportunities available.

What is the Impact of Taking a Gap Year?
AmeriCorps is a network of national service programs through which participants work in communities in areas such as education, public safety, health, and the environment. More than 50,000 individuals participate in AmeriCorps programs each year, many as part of a gap year.

A five-year scientific longitudinal study on the impact of AmeriCorps found "a powerful positive impact on members' attitudes and behaviors in areas of civic engagement, education, employment, and life skills, and that "people who take the AmeriCorps pledge and fulfill their year of service end up as more engaged citizens than they would have been had they not participated in AmeriCorps."

David Neidorf, director of the Integrated Studies Program at Middlebury College in Vermont, agrees that taking time off before or during college can have a positive impact on students. Middlebury students who take a break after high school are routinely called "Febs" (short for "February," as in students who start school in February instead of the fall).

When asked if there is an observable difference between Febs and other students, Neidorf said: "In general, kids who take time off have their stuff together. Febs are more mature and tend to have a better time because they know why they're in college, [they're] the kind of people who can work more independently and effectively. They don't get as frustrated with the communal aspect of college because they've had a chance to get a sense of themselves on their own. They don't have as much to prove."

Approximately 15 percent of the freshman class at Middlebury takes time off, and, Neidorf observes, "when they introduce themselves, they say 'I'm a Feb,' and it's a distinction they're proud of."

There are several areas of consensus among the parents, students, program specialists, consultants, and researchers we've spoken with about the benefits of the time-off experience.

Greater confidence and independence. Students gain a great deal of confidence by taking responsibility for their destiny and by contributing to the welfare of others during time off. In the words of one parent whose daughter conquered the Appalachian Trail over a six-month break between high school and college (a feat achieved by only 10 percent of those who attempt it), "My daughter now knows she can do anything in the world!"

Passion for learning. Many students report that they discover or rediscover a passion for education and become active learners (in contrast to passively processing information that is fed to them in many traditional classrooms). Parents have noted that children returning from time-off experiences are more avid readers and writers. "Being in Costa Rica and teaching reinvigorated my work ethic completely. When I returned, I was ready to apply to college and take that step to move on," reports Mitchell Levene, a time-off student from

Dallas, Texas. Such experiences also can lead to validation or alteration of a life direction, such as what comprises the best match in a college or a career.

Perpective. Through exposure to other places and cultures and being "out of their comfort zone," students can develop a more mature perspective on themselves and the world and a greater respect for different cultures, traditions, and spiritual orientations.

Organizational and practical skills. Gap-year participants can learn to master life skills earlier than many of their peers. These skills may include cooking, cleaning, traveling with ease, living in diverse cultures and sometimes in challenging conditions, handling money, problem solving, and communicating more effectively. When Adam returned from living and working in an environmental preserve in New Zealand, for example, we were transfixed watching the former fast-food devotee cook whole wheat breads and vegetarian delicacies from scratch and even forgo using the dishwasher.

Taking things in stride. "Understanding there is a whole world out there has helped me take things in stride. I'm less affected by setbacks and shortcomings," stated one student. Being more relaxed and able to distinguish the important from the trivial can translate into less stress in college and other aspects of life when confronted with unfamiliar challenges.

In addition, time off yields memories and friendships that can last a lifetime.

What Do Colleges Think of Students Taking Time Off Before or During College?

For more than thirty years, Harvard College has recommended that students consider taking time off between high school and college. (A May 2000 article in *The Crimson,* Harvard's student newspaper, reported that students who took this advice found the experience so valuable that they would recommend that all their fellow students consider it.) Princeton has begun recommending in its acceptance letters that students consider taking time off before entering college.

Other schools have no official policy on time off before or during college but provide resources and information for students interested in these options.

The Venture Consortium (www.theventureconsortium.org), headquartered at Brown University in Providence, Rhode Island, invites colleges to sign up for their services, which include access to a database of jobs and support with time-off placements. Venture's member schools include Bates, Brown, Connecticut Wesleyan, Franklin and Marshall, Holy Cross, Sarah Lawrence, Swarthmore, Syracuse, and Vassar. The University of Michigan (www.umich.edu) has an international center that features information on applying to study and work abroad, internships, volunteering, teaching opportunities, and more.

With increasing pressure on colleges to report on-time graduation rates, it's unclear whether acceptance of time-off options among post–secondary institutions in the United States will grow. "I think when you have statements from Princeton and Harvard supporting this option, it will trickle down," predicts Holly Bull, president of the Center for Interim Programs.

Will Colleges Defer Students Who Take Time Off Before College?
Gail Reardon, founder of Taking Off, an organization that works with young people who are taking time away from the traditional classroom before, during, or after college, advises students to apply to school and defer admission. "Taking time

off is easier for students and parents when there is a system in place that includes college," reports Gail.

Most schools will grant a deferral if presented with a reasoned case and an idea of what a students plans to do or accomplish during the time off. The greatest risk in deferring admission to a specific college is that your child may develop firm and reasonable ideas about the best college match for him and her— and that match may not include schools that were of interest a year earlier. This might mean losing any financial deposit you have made; it certainly means gearing up to tackle the application process all over again.

Can a Student Improve His or Her Chances for Admission to College by Taking Time Off?

Several students we spoke with report that they were admitted to more selective colleges after participating in a gap year and being able to communicate the value of their experiences. This makes sense. Time-off students have an added dimension and maturity level that may give them a leg up on traditional high school graduates in the eyes of admissions officers. Experts caution, however, that influencing chances for college acceptance is a by-product, not a primary reason to participate in a gap-year scenario.

Can a Parent be Certain that their Child Will Go or Return to College After Taking Time Off?

This question is perhaps the most frequently asked by parents when considering a time-off option. It expresses their biggest concern. A college degree holds great significance for men and women in our society (portending better jobs, higher salaries, and greater social acceptance). It is easy to understand that parents may anticipate a worst-case scenario in which their son or daughter concludes there is such value in "real-world" experiences that returning to the classroom is unappealing.

It is a myth that "once you get off that train, you'll never get back on," says Bob Gilpin, founder of Where You Headed, a counseling service that assists students with researching and planning for a gap year. "Then there's the truth: it's a local rather than an express. You can get on or off as many times as you want to."

There are, of course, no guarantees in life except death and taxes (as the saying goes), but we can report that all the students we spoke with either have returned to college or have a plan that includes applying to college. The consultants, counselors, and program officers we've consulted affirm that, with rare exceptions, students return to school. In addition, they report that they are more focused on studying, more likely to appreciate the value of education, and participate more actively in their education.

Will Gappers be Out of Synch With Other Students When They Return to College Because They are Older?

It is true that time-off students tend to stand out on a college campus, but not because of an age difference. Being a year or two older generally is not an issue. Gappers are distinct because they have a set of experiences different from those of their peers; they tend to be more mature; they develop leadership and coping skills earlier than most of their classmates.

"The transitional issues are not around academics, but tend to be social," says Gail Reardon of Taking Off. "College students go through a bump when entering college, and time-off students can go through an extra bump. They see the world and themselves differently than their classmates. Taking responsibility for their learning when the world was their classroom gives them a sense of competence and maturity that makes a difference when it comes to connecting socially. Every freshman is looking for people with whom they can identify and connect so they feel they belong. Finding that connection when you have taken a gap year may just take a bit longer," continues Gail.

The confidence that is gained during a gap year can help put college transition in perspective. "I can bring something to the classroom that a lot of college freshmen won't, and that can only enhance the experience of that college," says David Miller, of Cambridge, Massachusetts. David was a scuba instructor in the Cayman Islands and taught in Central America during his break.

Another attribute that students develop during time off is adaptability. They tend to apply lessons they learned to transitioning to college. Once on campus, students will gravitate to others who have time-off experiences through networking, participating in community service activities, or living in international dorms. Time-offers also tend to spread the word about colleges that are "gapper-friendly." These institutions may be more focused on experiential learning, incorporate international programs, and allow students to develop unique majors. These colleges also may be places in which students are more actively involved in college decisions or are expected to work on campus. They may have implemented policies specifically to support time-off students.

What About the Money?

The issue of financing a gap-year or time-off experience is bound to be on one's mind as parents and students weigh their options. There are numerous scenarios.

A student can identify and design experiences such as hiking, bicycling, or exploring that can cost little or nothing. On the other hand, studying abroad and receiving college credit for successful completion can cost thousands of dollars; some programs offer stipends or tuition assistance in exchange for service. Working and fund-raising, of course, can be woven into a gap year to help pay the bills and save money for college.

Some families are in a position to pay for programs without sacrifice, and other parents can offer no fiscal support. In any case, parents and their child should discuss financial implications, boundaries, and scenarios early on in the process. In almost all circumstances, students benefit from taking the lead in designing a year that includes saving money (through working or interning, choosing programs having stipends or that provide room and board, or by arranging for college credit for gap-year experiences).

In chapter 5, we devote more time to financial issues and share some tips for fund-raising and saving money.

How Does a Parent Learn More About Whether Taking Time Off May Be a Good Option for Their Child?
Turn the page and learn about the seven-step gap-year plan.

3

The Seven-Step
Gap-Year Plan

Experience is the father of wisdom, and memory the mother.
—*ENGLISH PROVERB*

THERE ARE ALMOST AS many reasons to pursue a gap-year plan as there are students.

The initial attraction may be the chance to explore the world—hike in the Rockies, travel in Europe or through Central America. It may be the opportunity to participate in community service or volunteer—do conservation work in Ecuador, improve literacy in Kentucky, or address health challenges in Africa. Or students may have the desire to save for college while gaining life experience—an internship with a political campaign, providing childcare in inner cities, or pursuing entrepreneurial opportunities in New York or Boston. The attraction may be educational, such as learning Spanish in South America, studying art history in Italy, or engaging in environmental studies in New Zealand.

Whatever the initial impetus, there is a universal recommendation from students, parents, and counselors: Have a plan!

Colleges, for instance, are more likely to defer admission if presented with a plan. Potential employers will value a well-thought-out strategy. You will sleep better at night if there is a structured sequence for your child's time off. Finally, and most important, your son or daughter will benefit from the process of developing and implementing a plan.

Many students report that the planning process is in itself a path to greater maturity and perspective. Making decisions and long-term commitments, weighing finances, working toward a goal, and reaching personal objectives along the way develop skills that will yield long-term benefits. Students report that these abilities:

- Prepare them to handle pressure and unexpected situations
- Teach them to deal responsibly with the relative freedom of college life (and with financial responsibility)
- Inculcate the discipline to study for tests and the confidence to participate in class
- Show them how to tackle long-term projects and independent study
- Lead them to become more involved in college life and the surrounding community

Parents say that having a plan—and supporting your child through decision making about gap-year options—can lay the foundation for a relationship that will sustain you both when miles and even continents separate you.

Business experts report that there are common attributes of effective planning. The planner should:

- Have a goal
- Keep it simple

- Make it flexible
- Know who's accountable

We have researched and designed a seven-step strategy with these characteristics in mind. The steps are designed as guidelines for you to consider and adapt, not as a rigid, linear procedure.

STEP ONE: COMMUNICATE

Of the students we spoke with, many report that talking to parents is the biggest hurdle they faced in deciding whether to pursue a time-off option. Melea Glick, a University of Toronto student whose gap year included service in AmeriCorps (www.americorps.org), remembers hesitating before introducing the topic.

"It's just that my parents had always assumed I'd go to college—it's part of their dream. I was afraid of letting them down and that they'd be disappointed in me." When digging a little deeper, students reveal that their concern stems in part from the fact that they have been on a lockstep treadmill for the most part from elementary through high school—and now the prospect of taking a road less traveled spurs a new and different set of questions and challenges.

Mitch Levene, a time-off student from Dallas, Texas, recalls, "Spending so much time in the education system can be draining. There was something about time away from academics that was invigorating. After taking time off, I was fully confident that I could succeed in college. I learned a lot of life lessons and gained a great deal of perspective because of the path that I chose."

Mitch, who had a powerful gap experience teaching English in a Costa Rican village, recognized during college application season that more school right away might not be right for him. "My close friends were much more involved and excited about the process than I was. When I didn't get into the schools I wanted to attend at the time, it was kind of the straw that broke the camel's back." He hesitated to tell his parents that he wasn't ready for college. At first, he recalls, "They were a little shocked." Once his parents realized he was going to do something worthwhile, they were on board. (His mother now insists she knew all along that taking time off was the right choice for Mitch, who is looking forward to attending Pitzer College in Los Angeles in the fall—"my top choice and a good match for me.")

There probably have been times when you believed that communicating with your teenager was an oxymoron (and your child probably has felt the same way about communicating with the 'rents'). Ideally, your relationship has grown beyond the awkward stage and you've established a basis for discussions around major life choices by the time of high school graduation. (As noted earlier, when we refer to "parents," in many cases we are including diverse and extended families that contain stepparents, guardians, grandparents, and other role models that teens may look to for guidance.) If, for instance, a student has participated extensively in extracurricular activities, worked while in school, or already applied to college, parents have gained experience as advisers and cheerleaders that they can draw on as a gap-year coach and supporter. However, if such a precedent has not been set, parents can use initial conversations about time-off options to open a constructive and mature line of communication.

In most cases, according to the parents and children we've talked to, the time-off option is introduced by the student. Will Hunt, who took a break before entering Middlebury College, thought through the time-off option before bringing it up to his parents because he wasn't sure of their reaction. "They focused me on getting into college first," which, in retrospect, Will views as good advice because "kids who have no direction before they take a break could end up going nowhere."

In some cases, parents will introduce the topic. Steve Wildman read about students taking time off in a *New York Times* article a couple of years ago. What he read made sense.

"Looking back, I regret that there weren't opportunities to take time off in my life. Back then, of course, there was the strong possibility of service in Vietnam in my future. Today, once you get out of college and are on a professional path, you don't have the same freedom and opportunity as between high school and college. The appeal of a gap year seemed to be that you mature, gain independence, and gain experience with other people and cultures. I believed that this could be an experience for our daughter that would stay with her the rest of her life."

As a professor in economics and telecommunications at Michigan State University, Steve also had the perspective of observing students who arrive on campus with very little direction. He shared the article with his wife and filed it away for when it made sense to plant the seed that this may be an option for their daughter, Brittany. During the process of visiting colleges in the fall of Brittany's senior year, the Wildmans talked about the time-off option. Their daughter was interested and began researching it.

Experts advise that, even at the initial communication stage, time-off discussions should involve the whole family.

"A time-off plan is not going to work if it's not a family decision," reports Gail Reardon, who runs Taking Off, a personalized program that works with young people interested in taking time off before, during, or after college. "But the teenager has to 'own it.'"

There are resources for parents and students interested in gathering more information on how to introduce the gap-year option. The College Board's Web site has advice for parents (go to www.collegeboard.com and simply search for "time off "). AmeriCorps has a brochure for teens on how to talk with parents about taking time off. (We've included additional resources in part 2 of this book.)

Once the conversation has begun, many parents recommend having questions in mind that can help mold the dialogue over a gap-year strategy. These can become an operating basis for joint decision making regarding college and other life choices in the year ahead. The focus of questions at the beginning of the process is to learn how your teen is thinking about the gap-year option as well as college. They can also help establish the expectation from the beginning that succeeding in college is an integral goal of a gap strategy. Such initiating questions could include:

- Why do you want to take time off before or during college? What are your goals?
- If you're taking time off in the year after high school, do you plan to apply in the fall of your senior year and, if accepted, defer college? If not, how would taking time off now help you decide where to go to college—and make the most of college when you go?
- What experiences have you had in life so far that make you think this is a good option for you?
- What research have you done so far about programs?
- Are you prepared to make the long-term commitment that this will require?
- What will you be giving up by not going to college right after high school?

- How will you answer those who say that you'll never go to college if you don't go now?

A topic that will inevitably be in the back of your mind—and your child's—even during an initial discussion about taking time off is finances. After all, paying for college is a major concern and stress for most parents and families. According to the American Express Educational Loan Survey, 70 percent of parents of high school–aged children say they are worried about their ability to pay for college. You may be wondering how taking a year off will cut into your savings (particularly if your child has already been offered an attractive financial aid package) or the impact it may have on younger siblings and their college plans.

Within a time-off plan, however, there are numerous financial scenarios. (Chapter 5 offers more information on financial issues and suggestions for fund-raising.) It should be expected that a student will take the lead in designing time off that includes his or her saving money (through working, or interning, choosing programs having stipends or that provide room and board, or arranging for college credit for gap experiences). Parents should be prepared to bring the financial issue up early and establish that all options are on the table. Your child likely will wait for you to outline the parameters and expectations, which may be that the gapper will raise or work for some or all of the needed money or that he or she will focus on less expensive or no-cost options. Some students report that their parents could provide nothing beyond "moral support" during their gap year, but that this was enough. Lack of up-front finances, they advise, should not be a barrier. Students also note that taking responsibility for the money increased their ownership and rewards from the time-off experience.

Pam Lassiter was hesitant when her daughter, Allison, first articulated the goal of taking time off between high school and college to hike the Appalachian Trail (a daunting 2,600 mile trek from Georgia to Maine).

Allison, however, had a strategy mapped out that included applying to and then deferring college. Pam listened to her carefully and recognized that the plan was well thought out. Allison was clear and persistent about her objectives over time. In addition, Allison's desire to conquer the Appalachian Trail was consistent with her lifelong love of the outdoors. Pam reasoned that her long-term relationship with her daughter had greater importance than her own reservations. She became a strong supporter of her daughter's experience.

As Pam's reasoning shows, the investment in listening carefully and constructive communication at this stage will pay off. Remember, you are beginning a discourse that has at its heart a process—maturation. You are helping your child to learn how to make important decisions and to explore the consequences of those decisions, which he or she will live with long after the gap year ends.

STEP TWO: AGREE ON ROLES AND RESPONSIBILITIES

Once the ice is broken and the gap option is on the table, many students report feeling a sense of relief and excitement. Adam seemed to mature before our eyes as he laid out his reasons why teaching and traveling for at least a year was right for him.

Parents report mixed reactions if they're not familiar with gap-year strategies (and it's not uncommon for husbands, wives,

stepparents, and other family members to have different re-
sponses). Others can draw on their own experiences in considering their child's interest in taking time off.

Donna Rubin's perspective as a college counselor at the
Rochester Institute of Technology enabled her, as a parent, to
support the passion of her son, Ben, when he sought to delay his
entrance into college. Ben's time-off plan included graduating
early from high school and devising a practical way to support
himself while pursuing his love of skateboarding in California.
Donna had seen many students flounder in college and had observed that those who took time off were more focused when
they returned. She observed that Ben matured during his year
in California as he managed the challenges of supporting himself through a number of part-time jobs and sharing an apart-
ment with four other young men. One sign of this maturity was
the way Ben took on his responsibility as a camp counselor who
taught skateboarding to youngsters prior to his admission to the
University of Redlands.

After initial conversations and processing initial reactions,
it's time for parents and their teen to put a time frame around
the plan that will move taking time off from a dream to a firm
option. Identifying roles and responsibilities is a logical next
step. The purpose of this is not only functional but to help ensure commitment from all parties involved.

If you're like many parents, you've had experience discussing
responsibility with your child in the past. It may have gone something like this: "But Dad! I really want a dog!" "And who'll take
care of it?" "I will! I promise! I really, really will!" You probably
know the rest of the scenario as you've found yourself picking
up the pieces and wondering how once again the roles and responsibilities ended up with you.

But your teenager is no longer a dependent child (and may

have demonstrated his growing capacity if he has presented you with a coherent, comprehensive plan and rationale for taking time off). He will need to tackle responsibility in a new and mature way in order to get the most out of a gap year. If you haven't already done so, now is the time to transition from a heavy parental role to that of coaching your child to take responsibility for planning and making the plan work. The traditional adult role of identifying issues, exploring implications, and assessing potential risks should increasingly be taken on by the person who will be living the experience—your teen.

Examples of the roles and responsibilities may include the following:

Student's Roles and Responsibilities

- Establish one or more goals for the time-off period
- Communicate openly with parents and others about time-off options
- Represent family, community, and (if traveling internationally) country in a responsible manner
- Take the lead in determining whether colleges will defer admission
- Apply or reapply to colleges (if appropriate) as a part of timeoff
- Pay strict attention to deadlines (e.g., for applications) and timelines
- Provide an early warning signal if problems or issues are likely to arise
- Work out a financial strategy that details his or her part in paying for the gap year and stick to it
- Reflect on and chronicle experiences

- Share reflections about his or her experiences (e.g., visit a class at high school, speak at a church or service club)
- Be reasonable and flexible

Parents' Roles and Responsibilities

- Have an open mind and respect your child's growing independence as he or she plans time off
- Keep your child's stated goals in mind and provide feedback on his or her progress toward these goals
- Maintain an open line of communication; deal with any conflict in an open and up-front manner
- Conduct your own research regarding programs, options, and issues (e.g., potential tax deductions, safety, program structure)
- Be a backup system and reminder regarding timelines and deadlines (you have more experience with details and are better positioned to monitor what needs to be done and when—and to coach or support your child when there are roadblocks)
- Take the lead in some details (e.g., health care, passports, double-checking program credibility) and keep track of documents
- Consider how your network of friends and contacts can help inform your child's experience (friends who have traveled to or have lived in the state or country your child is researching may be useful resources)
- Be reasonable and flexible

Some families choose to write their roles and responsibilities down in a "contract" that formalizes what they've agreed to. Whatever form it takes, the gap option entails commitments and accountability, important life lessons that parents can help impart as the plan takes shape.

STEP THREE: DEVELOP A TIMELINE

Steve and Susan Wildman took the lead in laying out a timeline for Brittany's break year. With a sequence of activities selected by Brittany that included time in New Zealand and Australia, working on a tiger refuge in Tyler, Texas, and conducting whale research in Maui, her parents reasoned that they were in a better position to anticipate deadlines and encourage long-range planning than their daughter (who had less life experience and, like many teenagers, could sometimes tackle what was in front of her only at the last minute).

A timeline, important for any plan, is a critical element of a time-off strategy. It will be a prime means of ensuring your teen is on track and accountable for implementation. A timeline provides a sense of urgency and countenances fewer excuses for procrastination. Timelines should establish important milestones, including deadlines for submitting applications, obtaining a passport for overseas travel, making reservations for travel and lodging, and the like.

The general timeline for applying to colleges is relatively well established and comes with built-in reminders from school counselors and colleges themselves along the way (take SATs or ACTs, mail the applications and financial aid forms, accept or reject schools, etc.).

The time-off plan, on the other hand, will have many layers and details. Confronted by this complexity, the parents may choose to enlist the assistance of a fee-based consultant. He will design an individualized time-off experience for your child and will assist with setting timelines and deadlines. (See box on pages 63–64 for more information on the advantages of using consulting services.)

If you are totally on your own, you may want to maintain a calendar to remind your family of key milestones and dates. Remember that, in many cases, early planning can open the door to cheaper travel, richer program options, and more selective internships and community service experiences—and otherwise save time and money. For example, some of the more competitive internships that have healthy stipends impose earlier deadlines and entail a more complicated application process than other programs. Some deadlines—as applying for health insurance for your child, if necessary, or getting a passport and visas—you can't afford to miss.

STEP FOUR: RESEARCH

"You had better research your program options and, once you know where you're going, research some more to be sure you know exactly what you're getting into," advises Erika Dickson, a premed major at the University of Michigan who dedicated her time off to teaching in a small village in Ghana. "I had a friend who did a program where she had to work thirteen-hour days at an orphanage because she didn't research her program carefully enough."

There are thousands of opportunities out there, and it takes serious work to find the best match for your child.

Many families are overwhelmed by the variety of programs and the options that are available, once they dive in. A student may have heard about AmeriCorps; she will find through research that there are hundreds of other opportunities for community-based service in the United States and abroad. She may have heard about Outward Bound (www.outward-bound.org)—and discover there are many additional ways to channel an interest in the outdoors into meeting leadership and skill development goals.

The process of discovery is almost endless. An obvious place to begin the search is the Internet. The Quaker Information Center (www.quakerinfo.org/oportnty.htm) has a free, searchable database of programs. Consultants and counseling services—such as the Center for Interim Programs (www.interimprograms.com), Taking Off (www.takingoff.net), or Where You Headed (www.whereyouheaded.com)—offer thousands of choices in their respective databases. (Part 2 of this book lists the Web sites of programs and resources. It should give you a good start.)

Research, however, doesn't end with merely checking out options. Your teen will want to talk to other students who have participated in gap programs, and go on to read articles and books about different cities and cultures. (Phillips Academy, better known as Andover, a private high school located north of Boston, has a rich Web site with a section on taking time off that includes testimonials from students who have pursued gap-year plans. See it at www.andover/edu/summerops/iytestimonials.htm.) Research might draw your student into more seriously considering his or her life direction: Is that passion really about the outdoors or is it a budding interest in environmental science? Does the urge to teach overseas point to an interest in community service or teaching as a profession? Does a calling to work on AIDS research in Africa reflect an interest in medicine or a desire to "get as far away as possible from the American way of life" for a while? There can be useful and healthy discussions of these questions. Many college students don't engage in such discussions until they are sophomores and are confronted with having to choose a major.

You will be naturally inclined to go outside the family for planning advice. You may have friends, colleagues, and relatives who have lived in or traveled to areas your child is considering. Use them. Teachers and school counselors, too, may have useful advice and opinions.

A parent's initial research will very likely focus on different areas than the child's. For example, the parent may want to know the track record of a program, the relative safety of a country or area, or the scholarships and other resources available to support a student. In fact, an important and enriching aspect of the search may be comparing notes with your child on your findings once the range of options has been narrowed.

Don't be surprised if investigating gap-year options is contagious! We've spoken to a number of parents who became immersed in exploring the variety of opportunities that there are for their child to conduct community service, intern, study, or travel during a gap year.

STEP FIVE: ESTABLISH PRIORITIES FOR SELECTING EXPERIENCES OR PROGRAMS

Once you and your teen have identified options for a time-off plan, various factors will influence your teen's decision about the ones he or she wishes to schedule or include. Do not be surprised to find that your evaluation of what constitutes a good match in a program may differ from what your teen values.

The following attributes could be a good priority checklist for parents in considering programs:

- *A solid track record.* You want to be sure that your teen selects programs that have proven themselves to be credible and reliable: they deliver what they promise, they are well managed, and they have a customer-focused staff. (You and your child are the customers.) You should be able to discover these qualities by reviewing program Web sites. (For example, does the site have a section for parents?) You also may want to talk directly to participants or their parents, so the program managers should be able and willing to provide references to alumni.

- *Orientation to the eighteen-to-twenty-four-year-old age group.* The program should be designed to meet the needs and maturity level of students who are of high school or college age, and the personnel should take their commitment to this age group seriously. It is a good sign if there is an open invitation to parents to contact the program with any questions and if staff members provide prompt, respectful answers before, during, and after the child participates.
- *A good content match—a focus not too broad or too narrow.* Is your child sure that whale watching in Alaska for three months is going to provide the perspective he or she needs? Or is there a related skill or competency that underlies the motivation (such as studying marine biology)? Establishing the proper balance between a "broad adventure" and a "narrow skill" may require a dedicated conversation between you and your child and additional research about program content and design.
- *Cost and finances.* As discussed in other parts of this book, finances should be an up-front and open issue. Keep in mind that when there is a fee to participate in a program—and even if the experience is free (hiking or biking, for example)—there are apt to be associated expenses such as travel, health insurance, and specialized equipment, and perhaps charges for college credit.

- *Balance among programs.* Consultants and students who have designed gap-year plans advise that one experience builds on the other. This is important when considering how best to sequence programs or activities. If your child's objectives include going abroad in the spring, then working during the fall to save money for travel may make sense. You'll want to look at the length and timing of options—programs can be as short as one week or as long as a year. You will need to identify experiences that match your teen's timetable (with some breathing room in between to process and reflect on the experiences—and, of course, to do laundry) and that complement each other. Programs shouldn't be redundant and should provide diverse experiences.

- *Sequencing.* The sequence of programs is important, and selecting the first experience may be the most important. Holly Bull generally recommends a structured, group-oriented program for first-timers or younger students (between high school and college). Such structure is a recommendation that many parents welcome. David Miller, a student from Cambridge, Massachusetts, recognized that the sequence of programs and the choice of a first program were important for a slightly different reason. "I needed to be away in the fall when high school is starting and all my friends were in college."

Parents recommend having another set of questions in mind once a range of options has been identified. This series is designed to probe what your teen anticipates will be the outcomes of the different activities, with a focus on how a series of experiences might work together in an overall plan. Communication at this point may focus on your determining how realistic your child's hopes are, again without making judgments, and providing feedback from your research or your own life experience. Answers here should not be considered binding, but will indicate if the plan as a whole hangs together in terms of your child's expectations and goals. Relevant questions include the following:

- Based on the research you have done on programs and experiences you are interested in, which ones are right for you? And why?
- Do the programs you have chosen build on each other? Which would you see yourself doing first?
- What is it that you hope to learn from each program that will help you get more out of the program that follows it?
- How will you measure success in a program or experience?
- How do the programs individually and collectively help you work toward your goals?

Jane Goldstone, the director of Global Routes (www.globalroutes.org), stresses the importance of finding the most appropriate fit for students and parents putting together time-off options. She suggests developing a matrix listing the kinds of factors that will affect program choices. Among these are the geographic location, the length of stay at one particular destination, the type of activity, and the level of supervision. For international programs, categories might include the degree of language immersion, the amount of travel, and safety considerations. Jane points out that if you are considering a program that involves a homestay (such as Global Routes provides), it is important to know how the host families are chosen and how closely the experience of students is monitored by program staff. Jane's primary recommendation in investigating options is to talk to program graduates and their parents to ensure that the program delivers what it says it delivers.

With a structured sequence of activities in mind and a timeline in place, many teens report that they feel liberated. Here it is well to remember that one of your commitments is to be flexible. It is likely that the plan will change as your child embarks on his or her adventure and learns more about the world and themselves. Once you have designed the gap year, sit back and take a deep breath because the nitty-gritty phase of logistics and details is about to begin.

STEP SIX: STAY ON TOP OF LOGISTICS AND DETAILS

Regardless of how responsible your teen is, you will find that many of the logistics and details will fall to you. This is because you have the experience and foresight to anticipate what needs to be done and when, as well as the know-how for troubleshooting when a challenge arises. In addition, your child may be unreachable (hiking a trail or out of the country) when the time comes to fill out and sign forms, transfer money, provide supplemental information for applications, or nail down travel reservations.

A commonsense way to stay on top of particulars is to document and keep records on contacts, travel itineraries, program information, and other details and to file them in a folder or keep them all in one place. Particularly in an emergency, you'll need all relevant information at your fingertips. In addition, you will want to keep detailed notes when you or your teen talk with personnel about program features, costs, and travel arrangements.

The process of identifying and tackling logistics and other details starts long before your child begins a program or activity, and it continues through the year. The work will require some patience. If there is not a specific program involved—if your child is going to be "out there" on his or her own—logistics and support may be even more crucial. Chapter 5 goes into detail about how to handle specific issues and part 2 of this book provides additional resources that should be of assistance.

STEP SEVEN: REFLECT

During the student's time away, the variety and depth of his or her new experiences can be overwhelming. Many students cope by keeping a journal or a diary to document their experiences and by taking a prodigious number of photographs.

"Keeping a journal through time-off experiences and the changes you go through is important, and I would recommend it," says Kathy Olson, who is with the United Way of the Midlands in Columbia, South Carolina. "What you go through can be profound. Through writing and reflecting, I was able to better track my thoughts, get a handle on the onslaught of activity, and process sometimes overwhelming emotions. It also helped me translate what I had learned for family and friends when I got back home."

Reflection is not just about looking to the past; it's about the processing of our experiences in the context of how they will impact the future and being able to communicate what we have learned to others. This important element will be integrated before, during, and after a gap year and will take place informally as well as formally.

You may get a sense of what your child is thinking and processing through e-mails and phone calls. (Parents we spoke with kept copies of e-mails and some took notes on phone calls to get a sense of how their child was processing experiences over time.)

Some programs formally incorporate opportunities for reflection. Outward Bound, for example, traditionally incorporates time at the end of each day within a weeklong program for participants to "process" the day's experiences. As the week progresses, leaders encourage participants to share insights with one another such as how they handled challenges they faced or how the group can work better as a whole to overcome obstacles. Instructors emphasize at the conclusion of the program that a goal of Outward Bound is to help participants see how lessons they have learned apply to their lives "back in the world."

Global Routes organizes participants into groups of up to fifteen volunteers for some of its programs. The groups meet for at least a week at the beginning of a multiweek program and again at the end to process and share experiences. Within the program, students are sent in pairs to villages in Central America or Africa to teach and also meet with the group at least once a week to discuss "values" and their struggles and successes.

Transitioning back home after gap experiences (particularly after immersion or homestays abroad) can be more challenging than anticipated, and we have devoted a section of chapter 6 to this issue. Part of reconnecting will be students sharing experiences through recounting stories of people they have met and offering pictures or artifacts from their journey. They may feel themselves coming down from a "mountaintop" experience and can be frustrated by the attempts to translate the highs of the experience to those who haven't been through what they have. A key recommendation to parents from talking with students is to listen and let your child process readjustments in her own way in her own time.

Students also will have mental snapshots of memorable moments that are difficult to translate into words. When you are together in between experiences, you can provide the opportunity for your child to share and offer reflections. "Choosing to participate in AmeriCorps was the first time Melea was internally driven to follow her dream instead of simply responding to external expectations of others, including her mother's and mine," said Gary Glick. "It was important from the beginning that she begin to incorporate into her thinking how to apply what she was learning holistically." This is not simply a matter of a child "bouncing back" to life as it was experienced before a gap year. She will be incorporating what she has learned and experienced as part of a process of growth and transformation.

As parents, you will have your own insights into the impact of the gap experience, based on communications over the time apart. Questions at this "reentry" stage can provide the opportunity for parents to help their child evaluate their time off in light of the initial goals of the year and to help integrate experiences into what comes next. Reflection includes considering the year as a whole and the growth that has taken place, the skills acquired, lessons learned, and relationships built or strengthened. Questions for parents to have in mind include the following:

- Did taking time off meet your expectations?
- Would you go back (to the country or place)?
- Will you stay in touch with people you met?
- Has your perspective on education changed?
- What are you thinking about college?
- What did you discover about yourself—what trait or characteristic—as a result of your experiences?
- What is your most memorable moment from your time off?
- If the child was part of a group program: Did you find

that some people in your group got more out of the experience than others? If so, why?

- Has your experience helped you focus or refocus on what you want to study in college?
- If you had to do it over again, would you do anything differently?
- Did you meet your goals?
- What advice would you give other students considering a gap option?

Students who have arranged to earn college credit for a gap experience will likely need to document their experiences. If your teen plans to reapply to college, he or she may want to translate what has been learned into college essays or scholarship applications. A number of gap alums return to high school classrooms to share reflections about their journeys.

The interaction between you and your child through reflection can positively impact your relationship in the years ahead and cement the common bond that you have formed through the time-off experience.

Parents report that at the end of their child's journey and even for years after, they look back at the gap year as a major turning point in their child's life and in their relationship. Melea's father says that now when friends and colleagues come around and ask the standard question, "Where is your child going to college?" he talks first about the personal growth his daughter realized during her gap year.

"There was a time when I almost cringed when I couldn't answer that my child was going to college," he recalls. "Now I respond, 'I have a better question—does your child know why he is going to college?' I, for one, can report with great pride that my daughter went in search of an answer."

Such can be the outcome of your active involvement in the months of reflection associated with a time-off plan. The investment in shared experiences of communicating, researching, planning, and being supportive can establish a basis of mutual respect that can pay dividends over a lifetime.

4

Gap-Year Options

People and experiences during time off opened doors and my mind in ways that going to school never would have.
—KATHY OLSON, UNITED WAY OF THE MIDLANDS, SOUTH CAROLINA

STUDENTS MAY APPROACH TAKING a gap year with a firm idea of what they want to experience and accomplish . . . or have no concept at all of what they want to do. At first blush, students and parents will be amazed and even intimidated by the thousands of options there are to include in a time-off plan.

In addition to the breadth of opportunities to perform community service, study, intern, and explore, students today live an era when they can travel with relative ease to any corner of the earth, e-mail and telephone service has never been more available or cheaper, and ATMs are readily accessible in cities around the world. There have never been more experiences available for young people, especially students in the United States, who arguably have more options than their peers in any other country or at any other time in history.

Where your child is along the continuum of choosing among

the many gap options will likely be tied to his or her motivation for stepping off the formal educational track.

Some students are drawn to seizing the unique window of opportunity presented by taking a year off between high school and college. When will a student have the same freedom to choose what he wants to do (after years of structure in the classroom and before heading to more years of the same)? The plethora of choices is wide open! Once in college, some students are at risk of burning out and, driven by that motivation, need a break. College students may be more likely to tie time off to their educational goals or questions about their direction.

Erika Dickson, as a sophomore at the University of Michigan, for example, found herself questioning what she was getting out of college (and was uncertain about having to choose a major) when she decided to explore options for teaching abroad.

Will Hunt from Providence, Rhode Island, "wasn't looking to change the world, but wanted to get out of his comfort zone" when he deferred admission to Middlebury College in Vermont to explore the world. "It may be the last time in my life I have this freedom," he realized.

Allison Lassiter's goal was firmly focused on conquering the Appalachian Trail when she postponed admission to Cornell University. She didn't anticipate experiences along the way that ranged from studying the impact of elk on their natural habitat in New Mexico to serving as a ski hostess in Utah, all in support of her goal.

As you and your child begin to delve into the options available—we've divided them into community service and volunteering, studying, exploring and traveling, and working and interning—the following questions might help to focus and narrow options.

Questions for Students

- Imagine it's a year from now: What do you hope you will have realized from your time-off experiences? Feel free to think big and dream large!
- Are there specific interests, goals, or passions you want to focus on?
- Are there areas of the country or world that you want to explore?
- Is one of your goals to get out of your "comfort zone"? If so, how far?
- Would you like to be part of a group experience (versus alone)?
- Are you interested in living with a family in another state, country, or culture (an immersion experience)?
- Is having English be the primary language spoken where you are a preference? How about another language?
- Is weather or a particular kind of environment (e.g., urban versus rural) an issue?
- Do you want to build travel into your year off (many students, in retrospect, wish they had dedicated more time to traveling)?
- Would you be interested in community service or serving others? If so, in what way?
- Do you have an idea for a first experience?

Questions for Parents

- Are you willing to pay for a gap program? What are your child's financial obligations within the time-off plan? Have you expressed and discussed financial limitations and expectations clearly with your child?

- Are you interested in using a consultant or counseling service to help guide your student through a gap year? (See the box below on "Consultants and Counseling Services" for more information.)
- Do you or another family member have the time and inclination to provide logistical support related to planning time off?
- What level of structure do you want your child to have during his or her experiences? (A more structured group program may be advisable for a first experience or for inexperienced travelers.)
- Will your student be reapplying to colleges during the year? Is time for this built into your planning?
- Do you have safety concerns about any particular type of experience or location?
- How much time do you have to nail down the first program for the year off?

Consultants and Counseling Services

Consultants act as partners, working with your family in developing a sequence of experiences that reflect your child's individual interests, goals, and unique characteristics. They charge fees—but most parents who choose to use consultants believe it to be a worthwhile investment. It may be worthwhile to talk to more than one to determine which is the best fit for your child.

Parents report that the advantages to using such services include the following:

- *Experience.* Reputable consultants have in-depth experience in the unique aspects of time-off planning and are dedicated to developing the best sequence of options for your child.

- *Program Knowledge.* Consultants can tap into thousands of program options and have personal experience and contacts with many of them.
- *Buffer Zone, Reality Check, and Neutral Third Party.* Consultants can serve as a neutral party who has no investment in what your student does during a gap year except to help figure out what makes sense. You and your child may not see eye-to-eye on time-off goals and plans; experienced consultants can provide a third-party view that you both value. From their experience with hundreds or thousands of students, they may be able to "read between the lines" and raise issues and options that may not be obvious and that you wouldn't think of.
- *Saving Time.* You may not have the time or patience to research the details associated with planning a gap year; consultants can save you time.
- *Intervention (If Needed).* In the event the unexpected happens (illness, bad program match, family emergency), consultants can step in, provide options, and facilitate action steps as necessary.

Even if you choose to use a consultant, there is no substitute for your hands-on participation and support during your child's time off. You don't want to miss out on the rewards you will receive through partnering with your child.

COMMUNITY SERVICE AND
VOLUNTEERING—UNITED STATES

Volunteering is second nature for most high school students. More than 80 percent have participated in some form of community service by the time they finish high school. Most have not, however, had the experience of combining community service with staying away from home for an extended period of time, living in a different geographic area, or becoming immersed in a culture that is a departure from their familiar routine. Within the United States, students can help rehabilitate wild animals in rural Texas (through LEAPNow at www.leapnow.org), organize a community housing project (through Habitat for Humanity at www.habitat.org), or teach English and outdoor education (through i-to-i at www.i-to-i.com or Global Routes at www.globalroutes.org, among many other organizations).

Students may participate in a strictly structured program or design their own options by approaching an organization of interest and developing an innovative solution to a challenge they want to tackle.

Advantages to Volunteering and Serving in the United States

- Build on community service or volunteer experiences the student had in high school
- Encounter fewer cultural barriers (familiar language, currency, laws, etc.)
- Take advantage of the vast number of places to visit and live in the United States and are able to "give back" in their home country.
- Develop an appreciation for other regions and subcultures of the country
- Travel with relative safety and security
- Need no passports or visas
- Spend less on their options, which are less expensive than international ones (with many providing a stipend, room and board, or other compensation)
- Stay in touch with family and friends more easily

Matt Hendren's Story of Community Service Through City Year in Massachusetts

Matt Hendren felt uninspired about going to college when he graduated from high school in North Carolina. During a school-related trip to Europe, Matt voiced uncertainty about his future to his government and politics teacher, Jonathan Milner. The conversation would change Matt's life. Matt listened as Milner and his wife, Cary, suggested there were alternatives to going straight to college after high school.

Cary shared the story of her own life-changing experience. Inspired by a book she had read on the life and work of Mother Teresa, she took time off after high school to work for the Kalighat House in Calcutta and cared for the sick and dying. She then hiked in Nepal and traveled in South India.

Seizing on the Milners' recommendation, Matt checked out the AmeriCorps Web site and ended up teaching fourth-graders in a rooftop garden in Boston's Chinatown through City Year (www.cityyear.org), which is affiliated with the AmeriCorps organization.

Spreading the ethic of service is now central to Matt's personal motivation. He is now inspiring high school students to take time off and is practicing what he preaches: he is working in City Year's development office for an extra year before entering the University of North Carolina at Chapel Hill.

"Coming to City Year was the best decision of my life," concludes Matt.

COMMUNITY SERVICE AND VOLUNTEERING—INTERNATIONAL

Phillippa "Pippa" King, from North Yorkshire in the United Kingdom, knew she wanted to "experience something completely different—to travel far from home and to learn new things through meeting new people and through different experiences. I knew I wanted to do a program and not just 'travel' and knew that I wanted to give something back and not have a selfish gap year."

For Pippa and students who share her passion to "get out of their comfort zone" as well as to give back, an international experience in community service and volunteering may be a meaningful segment in a time-off sequence. This option also will connect with parents who recall President Kennedy's challenge to participate in the Peace Corps (more than 168,000 Americans have responded to that challenge over the last forty years).

Within the international sphere, there are structured programs that offer community service experiences for students on most continents. Common gap-volunteer destinations today include Central America, South America, Africa, and East Asia. Service internationally can include teaching (frequently English, but other subjects as well), community development (building houses, supporting agricultural projects), or improving health care.

For parents, sending a child off into an unknown country for an extended period of time can be challenging and unsettling. "I was used to seeing firsthand what my children experienced," noted Wrenna Haigler before her son, Adam, set off for three months of community service in Costa Rica. "I feel it took great courage for my son to do something so different and fill his desire to serve. I didn't realize until I went there myself how different and difficult it is to live in an immersion situation in another country."

In an immersion experience the student lives with a host family in another country and culture while he or she works on a community service project. For many students we spoke with, the experience was one of the most rewarding challenges they had encountered in their lives.

Advantages to Volunteering or Participating in Community Service Abroad

- Get a chance to see the world
- Move out of their "comfort zone"
- Gain an in-depth experience that puts American life in perspective
- Learn how to live and move about in different cultures
- Learn how *others* live in different cultures
- Become conversant, or even fluent, in another language
- Make deep personal connections with people from other countries
- Establish a connection with the community they serve
- Learn to travel independently
- Take a break from modern conveniences (without TV, for example, students may find themselves reading and writing more)
- Have the satisfaction of making a contribution in an area of real need

STUDYING—UNITED STATES

The option of studying in the United States offers more of a departure from traditional education than appears on the surface. Students interested in delving into an academic subject in a hands-on environment (environmental studies in the Rockies, marine biology on Great Ships off the coast of Maine), testing out their attraction to the arts (attending film school in New York, trying acting in a community theater), or tackling something different from anything they were exposed to through formal education (culinary arts, furniture making) will find ample opportunity in programs throughout the United States—and, often, may earn college credit in the process.

Advantages to Studying in the United States

- "Get away" to study in a new environment
- Earn college credit (optional)
- Narrow down areas on which to focus in college
- Develop or maintain the discipline of studying
- Tie academic knowledge to "real world" experiences: they see the relevance of education
- Transition from a high school's structured experience to the relative freedom of a college structure and schedule
- Try out an academic setting or geographic location
- Interact with students from different backgrounds and regions of the country or world, and with different levels of academic preparation

STUDYING—INTERNATIONAL

According to the Institute for International Education, more than 160,000 U.S. college-affiliated students studied abroad during the 2000–2001 academic year (the most recent year for which there are data). Most study-abroad experiences combine instruction with exposure to the local culture and language and fold in related travel and, frequently, community service projects.

Kathy Olson recalls the advantages of her time studying art in Italy. "It was amazing to be able to go to museums and see the real thing—original works of art by masters or statues that were literally larger than life—instead of studying a one-by-two-inch picture in a book. The same with learning a foreign language through being immersed in a culture versus through books and tapes. Art was 'lost in translation' after my experiences in Europe." Kathy also volunteered in military schools while overseas, which she remembers as a first link with literacy and young people who were struggling with reading and writing skills. Years later, Kathy served as executive director of the Midlands Literacy Initiative, an award-winning program affiliated with the United Way of the Midlands in Columbia, South Carolina.

Some study-abroad programs are selective, with a rigorous application process, and others are less discriminating. Studying abroad can be a more costly choice than other gap-year options. The cost of many such experiences is equivalent to that of attending private college in the United States, and there generally are application fees as well as costs associated with obtaining college credit. However, with research you can find programs such as AmeriSpan (www.amerispan.com) that, starting at $700 for a language class, offer a relative bargain.

Advantages to Studying Abroad

- See and learn from original sources that aren't available in the United States
- Interact with students from a variety of countries and cultures

- Gain perspective on how education is done overseas
- See the connection between education and other aspects of a host country—museums, historical sites, and political/social institutions
- Gain a worldview that many American students don't have
- Learn or develop fluency in a language
- Find time to travel and explore

Scott Taylor's Study-Abroad Experience at Oxford University

Scott Taylor had applied for early decision at various colleges and was tackling three Advanced Placement courses the spring semester of his senior year of high school.

"Scott always had a great deal of confidence in himself and was floored when he didn't get in" to the college of his choice, his mother, Bobbi, recalls. After consulting with the Center for Interim Programs, Scott chose to attend Oxford University and participate in tutorials (two or three students per class) on British common law and international relations. He also was able to land an internship in the British parliament and ended up playing on the Oxford lacrosse team as well as hanging out with Rhodes scholars. Part of Scott's motivation in choosing to study abroad was to demonstrate to colleges—and to himself— that he had the capacity to study and earn good grades in a competitive academic environment. The Oxford experience exceeded expectations reports David Taylor, Scott's father. "In November, he called us and said, I'm on an academic roll . . . I can really see the value of education!" He had a thirty-minute international call with the director of admissions at Hampden-Sydney College in Virginia (his first choice) and "turned in his application on Monday and was accepted on Wednesday," according to Bobbi.

Scott had a successful first year at Hampden-Sydney and plans on studying international politics.

Bobbi reports that her son's time-off experience has led her to pose a different question to parents whose kids are about to graduate. Instead of asking, "Where is your child going to college?" she asks, "What is your child planning to do after graduation?" She uses these opportunities to share the idea that going into higher education immediately after graduating from high school is not the only option.

"You just don't know what good things can happen when you put yourself in a different situation from what's expected," adds David Taylor.

EXPLORING AND TRAVELING—UNITED STATES

What student hasn't had the urge to explore and travel in the United States? It can be natural and inexpensive to hike, bike, or camp in any of our fifty states. As with any time-off experience, however, it is recommended that the activity be tied to a goal or a personal growth journey. Students, for example, have raised funds for a charity by biking through northeastern states. Others have set out to study and document flora and fauna in a national park or forest.

Information on trails and parks is readily available through the National Park Service Web site at www.nps.gov. Parents may want to double-check that students have safety and emergency information, appropriate training (for mountain climbing, for example), and strategies for staying in touch. Outward Bound (www.outwardbound.org) is a structured, fee-based program that is well known for attracting individuals who want to develop skills and test their endurance.

Allison Lassiter Takes On the Appalachian Trail

Allison Lassiter set a goal of hiking the Appalachian Trail—a 2,600-mile trek from Georgia to Maine that only 10 percent of challengers succeed in finishing—in between high school and college.

At first, her mother, Pam, was hesitant. There were recognizable dangers involved in such a quest. "As competent and disciplined as Allison is and was, I couldn't imagine a nineteen-year-old female out there—alone!"

But Allison had mapped out a strategy that included applying to and deferring college (she had been accepted to the Ivy League college of her choice). As Pam listened to her daughter's plans, she saw they were well thought out and that Allison was clear and persistent about her objectives. Allison's desire to conquer the trail was consistent with her long-time love of the outdoors.

Since the six-month hike couldn't start until April, after the winter snows had melted, Allison had eleven months to fill after high school graduation. Her parents believed she would support herself, and she did. She networked herself into jobs such as landscaping on Martha's Vineyard and serving as a ski hostess in Park City, Utah. Allison also studied the effect elks have on vegetation through the Student Conservation Association (www.thesca.org).

Once her daughter had hit the trail, Pam found herself immersed in planning details such as how to ensure Allison had food to sustain her during the journey.

"Every ounce counts when you are packing for an excursion like this," recalls Pam, who mastered the art of dehydrating food that she would forward to strategic stops on the trail for Allison to retrieve. Allison's mother and father also joined her for several days of hiking after picking up the trail in Harpers Ferry, Virginia.

Looking back, Pam Lassiter is not only an avid supporter of the time-off experience but speaks with overwhelming pride of her daughter's accomplishments, which peaked with her conquest of the trail. "I'm in awe of what she did. I have incredible respect and admiration for her choosing a path so far beyond what I would have done." Pam, a highly successful outplacement human resources consultant and best-selling author, also says that she herself grew during the time-off process. "I can more easily accept what is and go with the flow."

"I think Allison's plan shows you can have it all—earn acceptance at a top school and take time off to realize a passion," Pam concludes.

Advantages to Exploring and Traveling in the United States

- Become acquainted with the natural resources and national parks of the United States
- Interact with nature and the outdoors
- Learn how to research and plan a route or itinerary and handle the related logistics (if designing activities from scratch without a formal program)
- Develop flexibility in regard to timing (may not need to book travel reservations in advance or apply for credentials, passports, or visas)
- Save money (these options can be relatively inexpensive, if not paying for a program)
- Use structured programs that are relatively short (one week) and fit them as modules into a broader time-off sequence of events
- Involve family members and friends more easily in some part of the experience

EXPLORING AND TRAVELING—INTERNATIONAL

Global exploration and travel can be added to the beginning or end of a structured international program or it can be designed as an end in itself. Dana Swanson, for example, decided, after a year of college, "I would rather be traveling the world than taking math tests," so she arranged to study Spanish in Salamanca, Spain, for a month and then set out to explore Europe. Her exploration of Europe was possible, she says, due to the confidence she developed in her traveling ability during an earlier supervised group experience in Central America. She went to Morocco, Portugal, Kosovo, Bosnia, the Balkans, Germany, the Netherlands, Poland, Great Britain, and France and says her time off could lead to a career in international relations.

Parents may have legitimate concerns about their child (even if an experienced traveler) venturing to areas of the globe with questionable safety status without a well-researched and well-planned itinerary. (More about safety, health, and related resources is provided in chapter 5.) A number of programs that offer structured, supervised, and group travel are included in part 2.

Advantages to Exploring and Traveling Abroad

- Test travel and communications skills
- Have the experience of being independent and responsible for themselves
- Travel to places that larger groups cannot go to (if traveling alone or in a small group)
- Have the chance to connect with the country or culture of interest or origin

Traveling Alone Abroad

We asked Adam to describe the experience of a student traveling alone when in another country.

"Traveling alone abroad can be an immensely powerful tool for developing confidence and 'road warrior' status. I traveled alone in Costa Rica for a month or so after my two structured programs in New Zealand and Central America. After having been supervised for six months (not to mention the eighteen years I spent at home), I felt the need to strike out on my own a little bit more, this time, alone. Being solitary in a foreign country is in a category all to itself in my opinion because you become, at some point along the way, your only friend. This is a point when introspection becomes a pastime and learning about yourself is a daily if not hourly occurrence.

"When you get tired of being in your own head, you get the chance to make new friends, because traveling alone allows you to connect with people that you would never meet with a group or even if you had just one friend with you. Your instinct to connect with anyone during a solitary journey may lead you to a new, lifelong friendship. I think that traveling alone, although it was for a short period of time, was one of the most significant parts of my year.

"After having used support systems when traveling, you feel a certain anxiety when you try it out for yourself and see where the wind will blow you. At least I know I did. So, parents, before you let your own fears dictate whether your child can travel alone or with a friend, think of all of the invaluable things they may learn along the way."

WORKING AND INTERNING—UNITED STATES

Earning money during segments of a gap year is an obvious and even necessary choice for many students. They may work in a familiar occupation (falling back on food-service skills learned in that part-time job in high school) or intern in a new and different work environment. (Bill Gates, for example, was a Congressional page, while Brooke Shields interned at the San Diego Zoo.) Students right out of high school can land responsible positions in public, private, and nonprofit organizations.

With enough planning, students have the opportunity to work or intern in a position that can complement educational interests or allow a student to "try out" a career and get a sense of what responsibility and accountability connotes in the "real world."

One program that specializes in finding paid jobs and internships for students affiliated with member colleges is the Venture Consortium. Venture offers a searchable database of job leads, internships, summer jobs, and other opportunities. Headquartered at Brown University in Providence, Rhode Island, member schools include Bates, Brown, Holy Cross, Franklin and Marshall, Sarah Lawrence, Swarthmore, Syracuse, Vassar, and Connecticut Wesleyan.

"Many employers dedicate individual attention to the placement and development of interns," says Peggy Chang, director of the Venture Consortium, who took time off when she was a student at Brown University to work through the College Venture Program.

"Every student who has come through this program has brought so much to the School," writes a representative from the Children's School on the Venture Web site (www.theventureconsortium.org). "In return, careful thought is given to what the School can give back to each intern, particularly in regard to personal and professional growth. A budget is set and discussed to plan for each student's development, whether it be course work, workshops, or designing programs for classroom curriculum."

Interns also provide valuable assistance to the organizations they work for, and, in many cases, the not-for-profits depend on them.

"Without our interns, our organization would sink," writes a staff member of the Glen Helen Outdoor Center in Yellow Springs, Ohio, on the Venture Web site. "The interns are responsible for educating the children who come through the center about the outdoors. Since we run an academic internship, the interns have to complete reading assignments, prepare lesson plans, perform peer observations, and complete a major project during their stay."

A good place to start your research on work and internship options is the searchable Internet databases that are geared toward young adults (see part 2 for resources). Networking among family and friends, of course, is a time-tested way to develop options and nail down a job. Enterprising students can create their own internship opportunities by approaching an organization and "making the case" that their services are needed.

Advantages to Working and Interning in the United States

- Earn money for a gap-year experience or college
- Build a résumé
- Try out a career field
- Encounter positive professional models to learn from and emulate
- Make professional connections that may be valuable in later years (when looking for a "real" job)
- Learn about different work environments and determine whether they are a good match for his or her talents, personality, or interests. (Some people find working at a

computer for an extended period of time satisfying; others would rather work in an outdoor environment. Some like working alone; others, in teams.)

WORKING AND INTERNING—INTERNATIONAL

If the goal is to work overseas for an extended period and earn a good salary, your child may be out of luck. Can your child get a work permit? In many cases, the answer is no, which means that he or she won't be able to work legally abroad. However, this depends on the country and the length of time he or she wants to work overseas. In addition to being knowledgeable about legal issues, an international worker should have a high level of ability in the local language and cultural fluency and will be expected to act in accordance with relevant customs, laws, rules, and regulations (which can be a tough act for students).

If the student's goal is to make and save money through working abroad, he very likely will fail. Consider that travel, living, and entertainment expenses depend in part on currency exchange rates. In Europe and Japan, especially, costs can quickly eat through a student's salary.

Even with all these caveats, students have found opportunities to live and earn a stipend (if not a living wage) in some reputable occupations and by working short stints as a nanny or au pair, a counselor at camps, a teacher, or on cruise ships, or even as a scuba instructor.

There are organizations such as BUNAC (www.bunac.org) that will help individuals find jobs in selected countries and will assist with work visas. However, they tend to be focused on setting you up in the job; support thereafter may be limited.

A more realistic plan is to focus on programs that combine a short-term internship with travel, cultural exchange, or study. AmeriSpan (www.amerispan.com), for example, specializes in international cultural exchange and invites clients to choose specialized programs in health, education, or international business. The Foundation for Sustainable Development (www.fsdinternational.org) offers both internships in developing countries that can translate into college credit and work-study tours that focus on a topic such as economic development.

Advantages to Working and Interning Abroad

- Gain practical, hands-on experience in a work environment
- Have the opportunity to explore career options
- Experience another culture
- Earn some money (if in a paid job or internship)
- Build travel around work or internship

After your student has settled on an overall plan and focused on a sequence of experiences, the next step is to tackle the logistics—travel, insurance, credentials, and other details—that are addressed in the next chapter.

5

Logistics

My parents' role was large and kept growing during the year.
—*David Miller, Cambridge, Massachusetts*

No matter how independent your student is, chances are you will get involved in logistics around his or her time-off plan. "Students in this age are more likely to ask for help and lean on parents than those of a generation ago," observes Betsy Hansel, who has twenty-five years of experience with time-off programs through AFS Intercultural Programs, Inc.

We cover a range of logistical areas in this chapter, from applications to budgets and fund-raising, exchange rates, travel, insurance and safety issues, among others. Some of our recommendations may appear to be plain common sense, but there may be other tips and resources you haven't thought of that can help save time and money.

WHEN TO APPLY AND APPLICATIONS

While experts advise "the earlier the better" when it comes to re-searching gap plans, the reality is that most students do not en-gage the idea of a gap year until the acceptance letters from colleges land at their door in mid-April. "I would advise families to have the conversation in February of the senior year, if not earlier, instead of waiting," recommends Bob Gilpin, founder of Where You Headed (www.whereyouheaded.com). "The trend is to wait until after college acceptances come in." Then it's busy season for programs, consultants, and colleges through early June as they work to assist students with placements, de-ferrals, and related details.

If you are considering programs that cost money, additional research can save you valuable resources. The most expensive program isn't necessarily the best. What is included in fees can also vary significantly. Some costs cover just tuition, while other programs cover travel, insurance, and other potentially expen-sive items.

When applying, a first step probably will be downloading an application from a Web site or e-mailing the program that will then follow up with you. Check each program for specifics on deadlines and what each application requires. There is no sub-stitute for talking directly with program staff, who should be ready and willing to answer your questions in a timely and re-sponsive manner. Hold on to the name, e-mail address, and phone number of your primary contact.

"When I called Global Routes, they always had someone available to talk to. Everyone was great to me, and I knew the whole staff by the time I left," reports Erika Dickson, who took the time to develop program contacts before she left for Ghana.

Your student may be eligible for scholarships or grants to

help offset program costs; be sure to allow enough time for applications to be processed if this is an option you'd like to explore.

In terms of complexity, many applications are relatively simple compared, for example, to college forms. There are selective study-abroad programs, however, that command additional thought and additional documentation (transcripts, recommendations) to meet admissions requirements. Many programs have prerequisites such as age requirements, high school graduation, affiliation with a university, or working familiarity with a language. Applications also may have sections for parents to fill out, particularly in regard to younger students. Employment may entail a more thorough selection process, including background checks that take time.

In some cases, a program your son or daughter is interested in will not materialize or will fall through. Given the number of options to choose from, a rejection isn't the end of the world. Chances are your child will end up with a program that matches his objectives and personality just as well.

Parents may want to be a backup for monitoring mail, phone calls, and e-mails regarding applications and placements when their child is on the road. Adam had applied to work in a conservation program in New England and initially was turned down and placed on a backup list. When the call came that there was an opening for him if he would call back within forty-eight hours, he was in Costa Rica and wasn't able to return the call until a week later. (He ended up with a better work opportunity teaching through The Outdoor School in Texas.) You don't want an acceptance letter with a deadline sitting in a pile of mail for several weeks or a request for additional information to go unanswered. If there is a rejection in the mail, your child also will need this information in order to line up other options.

The best advice when it comes to applications: Apply early, be persistent, follow up with program staff, and recognize that there are alternatives in the event first choices don't work out. Remember, flexibility was built into your original plan and will remain a guiding principle throughout.

Tips

- Compare and contrast programs
- Talk to participants and parents
- Have a contact on the program staff
- Let the student obtain and complete the application
- Be a backup for application follow-up if your student is going to be hard to reach

COLLEGE DEFERRALS AND CREDIT

Your student should take the lead in determining if a college will defer his or her admission, but this is an area you may want to monitor and provide extra support, if necessary. (We heard from parents whose children approached colleges to request deferral on their own and were initially turned down. When parents stepped in and helped make the case that the student had a solid rationale for taking time off as well as specific plans and goals, the deferral was approved.) As noted in chapter 2, your child's ideas about the best match in a college may change during time off. In this case, if a deferral is granted and your student chooses to attend a different school, you risk losing any deposit.

Don't count on earning college credit for an experience unless you are affiliated with a college or university and have specifics worked out with your home institution. Even if a gap program claims on its Web site or in its literature that "fifty colleges have granted credit" to participants, you need to work out and document details with a specific college. When credit *is* granted, extra work likely will be required (keeping a journal, writing a paper, etc.), which can be well worth the investment of time when weighed against tuition costs.

BUDGETS, FEES, AND FUND-RAISING

A budget will ideally be laid out within the parameters of any agreement you've reached with your student about financial roles and responsibilities. Some parents outline a budget upfront for their child to work with. Others agree to pay for half of time-off costs if their student raises the other half. Many students are on their own, although parents may provide advice and even help with fund-raising.

When considering a budget, a focal item will be direct program costs or tuition, if any. Even if there are no costs or you are being paid for an experience, there are other finances you should factor into your planning. These may include:

- Travel (and travel insurance, if appropriate)
- Housing
- Health insurance, immunizations, and medications
- Food (Will you be eating out, or growing and cooking your own food?)
- Passports, visas, or other credentials
- Staying in touch (e-mail accounts, phone cards, phone plans)
- Supplies, special equipment, and wardrobe
- "Nice to haves"—camera, journal, tape recorder, books

- Presents (if staying with friends or a host family, for example)
- Side travel and entertainment
- Laundry (if using a Laundromat)
- Emergencies

Don't forget to factor in *cost-of-living differentials* (even within the United States, there's a wide difference between living in a major city and a rural area) and *exchange rates* (if your student is looking at an international destination). After you've established a budget, consider ways to cut back. An International Student Exchange ID Card (www.isecard.com) is an internationally recognized ID and discount card available to students between the ages of twelve and twenty-six and can help cut travel costs. You may be able to borrow equipment, purchase secondhand goods, or offer trade-ins for upgraded supplies.

A Note About Program Fees and Exchange Rates: Parents and students should pay extra attention to documenting and confirming program costs and transactions when dealing with international programs whose fee structure is in a different currency than the American dollar.

We were surprised, for example, to find that one program's fees jumped within a six-week period by 25 percent, according to staff, due to fluctuations in exchange rates. (Some program Web sites note the potential impact of the exchange rate on costs and provide a limit to the amount the fee can jump.)

In addition, we had the experience of a program charging the total fee on a credit card when our verbal agreement on a phone call had been to charge just an initial deposit.

You or your child also may want to check out where tuition fees are going. If a not-for-profit organization claims it is devoting a portion of fees to community-based initiatives, is that really where funds are directed? A breakdown is sometimes provided on Web sites or is available upon request.

In the United Kingdom, there is an evolving initiative to promote the best practices among time-off programs. The Year Out Group was formed in 1998 "to promote the concept and benefits of well-structured year-out programmes [British spelling], to promote models of good practice and to help young people and their advisers in selecting suitable and worthwhile projects." Through the group, operational standards have been developed in areas that include planning placements, monitoring placements, and measuring customer satisfaction, as well as refining and improving processes. We are not there yet in the United States, nor is most of the rest of the world. So, until then, take extra care in double-checking fees and documenting what you are ultimately charged—and watch those exchange rates.

A Note About Tax Deductions: Did you know that some fees for time-off programs may be tax deductible? This fact is displayed on some not-for-profit program Web sites and, in Part 2, we've included this information for the programs where it is readily available. Global Service Corps (GSC at www.globalservicecorps. org) for example, states on its Web site: "All program fees (including airfare) are entirely tax deductible in the U.S. for U.S. citizens to the full extent of the IRS regulations." It points out that this means that, if you are fund-raising, family members, friends, and others "can make tax deductible contributions to GSC which can be directly applied to your program fees."

We discovered that a program Adam participated in during his time off had fees that are, indeed, deductible, but we were able to confirm this fact only after pressing the staff to research the issue. It would be a good idea for programs to research and provide this information to American taxpayers, but, in the meantime, it doesn't hurt—and may save money—to ask. Check with your accountant or other tax professional for specific applications.

If you consult a tax professional, remember to ask about the implications of any funds earned during time off. If a student is a volunteer overseas, for example, and earns a stipend, this may count as income that must be reported to the IRS even if a W-2 or pay stubs are not provided.

Tips

- Agree on budget parameters and responsibilities with your student
- Build cost-of-living and ancillary or extra fees into your budget—for travel, health care, entertainment, and emergencies
- Document conversations and correspondence about program fees
- Compare the relative costs of programs
- Understand what you are paying for and where the money is going
- Watch the exchange rate
- Dig for tax deductions

HANDLING MONEY ON THE ROAD

How you choose to handle money when your child is away may be similar to how you address the issue when your student is in college and based on your child's demonstrated experience with handling money as well as general maturity. Students may take the lead and decide independently how he or she accesses cash and processes financial transactions. In this case, you may want to just be sure they know the basics and understand any risks (e.g., what to do if money or a credit card is lost or stolen).

However, other parents make sure their child has traveler's checks or that their child has obtained a credit card for pre-scribed or emergency uses. If you are depending on him or her to access cash through a checking account, determine how your student will be able to retrieve funds where he or she is going. (It may seem to Americans that ATMs are ubiquitous, but they aren't everywhere, and transaction fees can vary, depending on the location or country). Traveler's checks, cash cards, and debit cards are other options for today's students. No matter how you decide to handle money issues, be sure you have a plan and discuss it with your child. Have a backup strategy in place in case of an emergency.

Some students may benefit from and value guidance on how to keep money, credentials, and other valuables close and safe. A money belt, for example, can be convenient and provide an extra level of confidence and security, particularly during travel. It doesn't hurt to offer commonsense advice such as to not leave money behind in a hotel room or a passport or credit card out of your sight when in a public place. (Adam had money stolen from his hotel room in a foreign city—an incident that could have been easily avoided had he been more cautious and taken the precaution of not leaving it behind.)

Tips

- Know how your child plans to handle money during time off
- Have a backup plan for emergencies
- Offer reminders on safety and security

PAYING YOUR WAY THROUGH WORKING
AND FUND-RAISING

Once there is a budget and a program or series of activities, working and fund-raising may be in your child's future. This is a good thing. In Britain, it is assumed that students will earn or raise money to pay for at least part of their gap year. This is an integral part of the time-off experience, and it is assumed that taking on this responsibility can be a valuable education in itself.

Before applying for jobs or checking into fund-raising options, make sure your student has determined whether he or she is eligible for any scholarships or grants offered by a specific program. Fill out any application accurately, completely, and on time.

Working and saving money may be the easiest way to fund a gap experience. Most students have had a job by the time they graduate from high school, whether it has been part-time work, babysitting, doing lawn work, or more substantial employment. Drawing on these experiences, students can save impressive amounts of money (particularly if they don't yield to the temptation to spend what they've earned while waiting for a time-off adventure to begin!). Students may search for jobs that help prepare them for experiences ahead (working in a camp to develop outdoor and teaching skills or working in a business where they can use a foreign language, for example). If fund-raising is part of your strategy to support time-off costs, it can be an advantage to also be working. Through having a job, you can demonstrate that you are working hard to reach your goals and people may be more willing to help.

Most students and their parents have experience in raising

funds for school-related projects—for sports teams, class trips, and the Scouts. This time, however, the mission is more personal, and the upside higher for your student and those touched by his work during time off. A main challenge, as with other aspects of taking time off, is to allow enough time to develop and implement a fund-raising strategy or project.

Fund-raising students should be professional and prepared when approaching potential supporters. They have to be able to "make a case" for why they are a good investment. (We pointed out above that donations for some programs may be tax deductible for supporters—a good selling point to an individual or business that a student should be able to document.) Students have opted for traditional fund-raising strategies or have been wildly creative in how to support a gap experience. On the traditional end, students can talk to local businesses about their plans and vision and appeal for their support. For example, they may approach an outdoor store about a conservation expedition in which they are participating and ask them if they can help out with a few necessary supplies. A local arts organization may have supplies or a few extra dollars for a student going abroad to develop his or her talent.

There are thousands of grant-making organizations and other nonprofit entities that may be willing to provide some support in accordance with their guidelines and deadlines. If you don't have direct connections with a community-based foundation, you will need to search for appropriate organizations and spend time on those likely to yield results. Obtaining grant money, however, can require lengthy applications and long deadlines for approval.

A student may consider developing a flier or a Web site to lend credibility to his or her time-off goals. Writing a letter to the editor, an op-ed piece, or a column for your community or local newsletter also can provide an element of authority to fund-raising efforts.

Students have initiated or leveraged events that can help their cause. A bike-a-thon or walk-a-thon, for example, can be a visible way to gain sponsors and get greater attention in your community. If a group of students in your community is planning on time-off adventures, they can join forces to stage an attention-getting event.

Additional recommendations for fund-raising from time-off veterans: Have a yard sale; make and sell T-shirts or food; throw a party with donated goods and charge admission; initiate a read-a-thon.

Students can appeal to family and friends for support. Adam chose to send a creative and enthusiastic letter explaining his time-off plans instead of the normal graduation announcement. Students also can tap into networks that might not be obvious at first—former scouting colleagues or inspirational teachers or mentors who helped inspire an initial interest in the passion that is guiding their time-off choices.

Another piece of sound advice is not to forget those supporters. Students need to take the time to thank them before they leave and follow up after they return. Personal letters explaining what was gained and the importance of the support will be appreciated and will help build the case for future students that investing in time off pays off.

"Financing a gap year doesn't have to be a chore if you look at it as a learning experience," one successful fund-raiser advises. "And it can be a way to meet new people who may come to care about who you are and what you want to accomplish in your community and in the world."

Additional resources available that provide tips for fund-raising are listed in part 2 of this book.

CREDENTIALS

Attention to detail and staying on top of deadlines is a good strategy for handling credentials.

You will want to allow time to process applications for passports and visas. For a first-time passport, a student will have to visit one of six thousand authorized facilities in the United States and supply two photos and a valid ID. A good starting place for additional details is the U.S. Department of State Web site at http://travel.state.gov—simply click on the "passports" or "visas" button on the home page.

You also will want to check expiration dates on driver's licenses, credit cards, health insurance policies, car registrations, and anything else having an expiration or renewal date in ample time to have the documents or policies updated.

Another type of credential to check out is the International Student Exchange ID Card. It can save you significant amounts of cash on travel, housing, and other activities.

Tips

- Research to determine the credentials the student will need (passports, visas, work credentials)
- Check all documents, policies, and credentials for expiration dates that might expire when your student is away
- Check to see whether a Student Exchange ID Card is to your advantage

HEALTH INSURANCE, IMMUNIZATIONS, MEDICATIONS, AND MEDICAL SUPPLIES

Determining whether your child's current health insurance policy will cover him or her while away should be near the top of your to-do list.

"A big challenge is to make sure there is health-care coverage," advises Bob Gilpin of Where You Headed (www.whereyouheaded.com). "Many big carriers are hesitant to deal with students who aren't in college. However, if a child is affiliated with an organized program, you can try to explain that they are doing something with the permission of the college they plan to attend. Sometimes that can be enough," suggests Gilpin.

You also will want to know whether dental or vision coverage is included as a part of an insurance package.

Check into health insurance issues early on. The application process takes time and can entail phone interviews or physicals (the latter, of course, is difficult to schedule if a student is on the road).

Short-term international insurance may be an option. It is reasonably priced (a quick search on the Internet should provide some choices). With any new or unknown insurance option, it makes sense to check with an insurance consultant to be sure that the policy is credible and provides a suitable level of coverage.

Program fees, especially for international travel, may include comprehensive travel or medical insurance. If so, refer to program Web sites for specifics on the types and levels of coverage or talk directly to staff representatives to determine what, if any, additional coverage you may need.

Immunizations or other health precautions (such as dietary or digestive aids) may be recommended for certain countries or regions. Find out what you need to know to make an informed decision about whether your child should get them.

Make sure that your child has an ample supply of any needed subscription medications or other medical supplies and a backup plan if they are lost or stolen while he or she is away.

Tips

- Determine whether an existing insurance policy will cover your student while not in school—whether the coverage extends to where he or she will be traveling
- If the student is affiliated with a school (e.g., there is deferred admission or an approved break), explain this to the insurance company—this sometimes makes a difference
- Leave enough time for application process (and any interviews or physicals that may be necessary)
- Check with an insurance consultant for options in your state
- Short-term insurance for international travel may be available—check the Internet
- Determine whether your child needs dental or vision coverage
- Check on immunizations and other health precautions that may be recommended
- Make sure your child has an ample supply of any medications (and a backup plan if a medication is lost or runs out)

PACKING

Many programs provide a checklist that tells the student what to pack (not unlike summer camp or colleges). However, packing for an extended stay far away from home or where there aren't modern stores or other conveniences can add an extra dimension to your planning.

First, be sure your student has researched the weather and climate at the destination for the appropriate season. Then check any limitations (set by the program or airline, for example) on how much she or he can take.

A general recommendation, as with most travel, is "less is more" when it comes to packing basic clothes, shoes, and accessories. There may be items that at first seem unwieldy that students can ingeniously pack or fit into a backpack. As presents for his host family in Costa Rica, for example, Adam managed to fit lacrosse sticks and a CD player into carry-on luggage. If you are planning to supplement luggage by sending supplies ahead or after your student arrives, be aware that shipping costs can add up quickly to some destinations.

Taking presents for significant people the students meet during his or her time off often is advisable—a lightweight and inexpensive token from your hometown can be meaningful and appreciated. Scarves, jewelry, key chains, coasters, sporting memorabilia, and caps are among the many items students choose as gifts.

Unless a student is certain that the time will be spent entirely in the wilderness or other area where there is no chance of having to present a "cleaned up" and appropriately clothed experience, taking at least one presentable outfit can be a plus. (You never know when you might be invited to someone's home, place of business, or community event where appropriate attire is desirable.)

Many students take a journal, camera, and an iPod or other source of music with them—and many who don't wish they had. There's nothing like being able to remember and share memories through your own thoughts at the time and pictures of the people and places you encountered.

Tips

- Check the weather
- Pack light
- Check with the airline or other travel company on limits to luggage
- Take presents
- Watch shipping costs
- Take at least one presentable outfit
- Remember the supply of medications!
- A camera, music, journal, and books may seem like extras— but can end up as necessities

COMMUNICATION

The good news is that communicating today is faster, better, and cheaper than ever before.

E-mail probably is the easiest way to stay in touch when your child is on the road. Make sure you have your student's up-to-date e-mail information (or start a group account to which your child can add an address).

The most effective and efficient way to stay in touch by phone will probably be through an international phone card or plan. (You'll want to research and compare plans based on the region or country your student is in.) In some cases, your child may figure out the best and cheapest method to stay in touch only after arriving at the destination. Snail mail can be just that—slow and even unpredictable when you are sending it to remote regions of the world, and packages can be expensive to ship. (As with college students, however, gappers will likely welcome a care package, photo selection, or other reminders of home.)

Even if your student is armed with the most up-to-date plans or phones, communication patterns will be difficult to predict. (See more on this in chapter 6.) Some students will be in touch more frequently and with greater depth than ever before, while others will want some "breathing room." You may want to establish a "chain e-mail" process so that your child can e-mail you and know it will be forwarded to a defined list of friends and family.

It is wise to follow the lead of your child regarding communication frequency and style, but be in touch yourself with positive, supportive messages whether via the Internet, phone, or post office.

Tips

- Check e-mail accounts and have accurate address at hand
- Research phone plans
- Check into using an international phone card
- Wait until your child arrives at his or her destination to see what works

TRAVEL AND HOUSING

A good rule of thumb is "the earlier the better" when it comes to nailing down travel arrangements. Particularly with air travel, early planning can help ensure the best fares (particularly around holidays) and help avoid blackout dates (for example, if you are planning to use frequent flier miles or coupons).

Take the time to compare and contrast different carriers and prices. A good tip is to look into the International Student Exchange ID Card—a bargain at about $25. It can save significant cash for eligible youth in travel, housing, entertainment, and more.

For national or international travel, Hostelling International (www.hihostels.com), with 4,000 hostels in more than sixty countries (including more than a hundred locations in the United States), is worth checking out. This is the same organization that has provided "safe, clean, and inexpensive" accommodations for young travelers for more than seventy years.

Tips

- Get an early start. Don't be blocked out of preferable travel dates—watch out for holidays.
- Look into getting an International Student Exchange ID card
- Have an emergency travel plan
- Use youth hostels—still a good bet

HEALTH AND SAFETY

Safety will be a concern of parents no matter where their children are headed or what they will be doing, regardless of how mature or responsible they are. It is wise for parents and their students to check into the situations, precautions, and what-if scenarios before deciding where to go and again before departing. Questions may include how safety and health issues will be addressed if health problems, accidents, or other emergencies impact an individual student or what will be done if there is a more widespread threat due to terrorism or political unrest in a region or country.

Many programs have a reputation for having staff and resources trained and prepared to handle safety challenges and emergency situations. We spoke with several students who became ill during their time off and who, with the guidance of staff, were treated and healthy within days. In one case, a student returned home for medical treatment—and was back on another time-off adventure within a month.

Of help here may be the Council on International Educational Exchange (www.ciee.org). The organization provides opportunities for individuals to study and work abroad; its Web site includes a section, "Health and Safety," that is an excellent resource for parents and students. It features information on CIEE's participant insurance coverage in the event of an emergency, its emergency preparedness plan, contact information for its emergency response team, orientation and training regarding risks and personal safety, among other information and resources.

CIEE offers the following recommendations designed for international travel that also may be applicable for domestic gappers.

Advice for Participants and Their Families
(Adapted from CIEE Web site)

- It is strongly recommended that participants designate their parents as emergency contact persons, unless specific circumstances require an alternate designee.
- Participants and emergency contacts should be in touch throughout a student's time away.
- Participants are responsible for ensuring their emergency contacts have current contact information at all times.
- In the event of any emergency (serious health problem, accident, etc.), participants should immediately notify their emergency contacts or have them notified.

CIEE points out that the U.S. Department of State Web site includes the following guidance: "Families in the United States whose U.S. Citizen relatives abroad are directly affected by a crisis can communicate with the Department of State through our Office of American Citizens Services and Crisis Management at 202-647-5225."

The Center for Global Education collaborates with colleges and universities around the world to promote "international education and to foster cross-cultural awareness, cooperation and understanding." Its Web site (www.lmu.edu/globaled/index.html) offers a "Student Study Abroad Safety Handbook," a clearinghouse, and other resources. It's "Top Ten Safety Tips" for students are:

1. Choose a quality program provider
2. Have adequate insurance and twenty-four-hour emergency assistance
3. Take care of your physical, dental, and mental health
4. Be able to communicate at all times
5. Avoid abuse of alcohol and use of illegal drugs
6. Make sure your mode of transportation is safe
7. Avoid crime and violence, including sexual harassment and assault
8. Be prepared to respond to emergencies
9. Avoid high-risk activities
10. Be informed about the country, city, and safety issues abroad

Health and safety conditions overseas can vary day by day and from country to country. Here are some additional resources for checking on specifics:

- Centers for Disease Control and Prevention's National Center for Infectious Diseases (www.cdc.gov/travel/index.htm). The Web site provides recommendations on immunizations, disease challenges, and other location-specific health information.
- Inter-Organization Task Force on Safety and Responsibility in Study Abroad (www.secussa.nafsa.org /safetyabroad). The Task Force was formed in 1997 by the Association of International Education Administrators (AIEA), the Section on U.S. Students Abroad (SECUSSA) of NAFSA: Association of International Educators, and the Council on International Educational Exchange (CIEE) to help "make study abroad as safe as possible."
- U.S. Department of State Tips for Students (http://travel.state.gov/studentinfo.html). This Web site provides information on what embassy and other offices can do to assist Americans who are abroad. It also gives medical insurance information.
- U.S. Department of State Travel Warnings and Consular Information Sheets (http://travel.state.gov/travel/warnings_consular.html). This site provides updates on travel warnings regarding security, political instability, or health issues in countries and regions

Tips

- Check safety updates on the destination. (The Web sites will provide a start.)
- Check the location and accessibility of local hospitals and other medical facilities
- Make sure your student is aware of your advised limitations on their travel

- Keep travel and medical insurance information, policy names and identification numbers, and copies of all relevant documents as backup
- Keep contact information, travel information, itinerary and emergency numbers in one place so you can easily put your hands on them, if necessary
- Have an itinerary and contact information if your student is traveling independently

6

What to Expect and How to Handle the Unexpected

Coming home was so much harder than I thought—Snickers bars here cost as much as a year of college in Ghana.
—*Erika Dickson, University of Michigan*

ALTHOUGH EACH GAP YEAR is unique, there are threads of experience that parents and students have in common. It was only in retrospect that those we spoke with were able to capture lessons they had learned through their time-off experiences. And, yes, there are times when time-off experiences entail challenges. "Even in the rare cases when the unexpected happens, time off is a universal learning experience," says Gail Reardon of Taking Off. "I have never, ever had a student or family regret it."

Some of these recollections are sentimental and many are humorous, but they all reflect the fact that young people grow and learn through their individual experiences and in their own way by taking time off.

We've organized our observations into the following areas:

- Countdown to departure and the first days away
- Communicating and staying in touch

- Living with a host family, or homestays
- Food (it can be more of an adjustment than you think)
- Readjusting

Several of these topics (such as what to expect during a home-stay) are of concern primarily to international gappers, but we have included them here in the belief that they hold value for all time-off students.

COUNTDOWN TO DEPARTURE AND
THE FIRST DAYS AWAY

"Nothing prepared me for the range of emotions I felt sending my youngest son off to a foreign land to live in a different culture," said one parent about the days before seeing her son off on his time-off adventure. "This was different than when a child leaves to college, which is an experience I can relate to and a place I know."

For some families, the days leading up to a student's departure for an extended stay in another country or for an alien experience in the United States can include anxiety for the parents and a "deer in the headlights" quality for students. For others, particularly those who have had experience with travel and staying away from home, the transition is like nothing at all.

To cope with anxieties, parents have channeled elevated energies and anxiety into bonding experiences—if they have not been consumed with handling last-minute travel details and related logistics. Some listen to language tapes with their children to help prepare them for living in a foreign land. Others have cooked a family meal featuring the cuisine of the traveler's destination before the departure date. Adam's mother interviewed him for an article for their church newsletter that focused on his dedication to service that he planned to apply in Central America. Pam and Allison Lassiter learned how to dehydrate food and measure it by the ounce in preparation for tackling the Appalachian Trail.

Once away, some first-time gappers experience homesickness. "The first month away for me was probably the most challenging part of my life—until the goodbyes when I left the kids I taught in Costa Rica and my host family," Adam recalls. "If you are not fluent in the language, there are no real communication lines in the beginning to your host community, not to mention host family, other than your broken Spanish. Loneliness is almost unavoidable. I thought about home and family every day for the first month and wrote in my journal about the rough times I was going through."

This is an area in which a structured group experience (such as that provided by Global Routes) has value. "With a first pang of homesickness, I worried about whether I would ever connect with my new country," one gapper recalls. "But I worked through it, and the program leaders who had experience with this sort of thing helped me work through it, too."

Students can find themselves reassured by reminders of home. Music had a striking impact on several travelers. "On really hard nights I would listen to James Taylor or Paul Simon and be comforted," recalls Laurel Wamsley, a student at the University of North Carolina at Chapel Hill, of her days in Africa. Mitchell Levene found himself listening to the Beatles, Bob Dylan, and Bob Marley in Costa Rica.

What You Can Do

- Recognize that feeling anxious in the days before departure (on your or your child's part) is an experience shared by other time-off families

- Plan or suggest family activities that a student can "take with him" while away
- Provide the opportunity for your child to express his or her feelings and emotions—if he or she wants to
- Suggest that the student pack photos, music, or other reminders of home for the "lonely times," if they come (or send them later in a care package)

COMMUNICATING AND STAYING IN TOUCH

Even though communicating is easier and cheaper today than ever before, the logistics of staying in touch during gap experiences can be tricky. Students may correspond through e-mail at school or from an Internet café, through phone calls or letters, and may keep journals, take photos, and even make recordings of their experiences to help impart their transformations.

"I expected communication to be easier. I figured I would talk with him every week and be able to track down what he was doing," recalls one mother whose son trekked into remote areas of New Zealand. "But there was no way to call him, and when *he* would call or leave a message, there was no way to call back. Phone calls when we connected became valuable." When a gap experience is taking place on the other side of the world, of course, families literally juggle night and day.

In addition to technical and time issues, staying in touch is influenced by individual communication styles and habits.

Some parents are pleasantly surprised that they hear more frequently from their child and that the messages have a greater depth than before they left. "No matter where I was, I was in touch once a week or so by e-mail or phone to share stories with my parents," noted one student. Others students, seizing on a first opportunity to be independent and focused on the present, will hardly reach out at all.

Students can be experiencing so much that it is overwhelming, and phone calls and especially e-mails can help them break down and process information more constructively. Most find creative ways to absorb and reflect their experiences.

"In the village everyone sits outside in the evenings," recalls Laurel Wamsley of her time in Ghana. "I would sit in the middle of the compound and write in a journal. The kids would come around me and watch. Then I'd start reading kids' books out loud that I brought from home. 'We came to learn' they would say . . . how many American teachers would kill for that moment? I'd never loved anyone as much as I loved those kids."

The way parents approach communicating is appreciated by students, particularly if they are positive and supportive and stay in touch even when there are lapses in return correspondence. Phone calls and e-mail exchanges can reflect the growth and evolving maturity of students: "I called my parents from New Zealand and realized they didn't treat me like a kid anymore," recalls David Roodhouse from Ohio. "They actually let me figure things out on my own and trusted me to do what I needed."

What You Can Do

- Don't have high expectations about the frequency or style of communications
- When you reach out through e-mails, be positive and supportive
- Keep copies of e-mail letters and even instant message transcripts—they can become a diary of transformations

taking place that can be reminiscent or humorous in the months and years to come

LIVING WITH A HOST FAMILY, OR HOMESTAYS

Homestays with host families can result in lifelong bonds, but initially they require adjustments.

"I remember coming home from Costa Rica and writing a letter to my host family, the Duarte Morales, the day I returned," says Adam. "I wrote in it, 'I don't feel like I'm at home anymore because I'll never be able to say that I have just one home.' Nobody can really understand what it's like to live with and be accepted by another family until they experience it. I could try to explain what host life is like, but my words could never express a milligram of the amazing love I feel toward my host family and community. I can honestly say that I have two families in this world."

Even the most positive host family match can require some initial adjustments, particularly when exacerbated by language and cultural barriers. In her first days in Ghana, Laurel Wamsley communicated through "a lot of body language."

"The first week my host mother woke me up at five in the morning to do housework with her and had me help with dinner and set the fire. She and I had some challenges because I am very independent." Laurel was used to jogging for exercise, a habit that seemed peculiar to her host mother. "She didn't want me to run, which was unusual to do for anyone in their village, much less for a female. Men would follow me on bikes and try to be my bodyguards."

In the end, Laurel established a deep and lasting relationship with those in Ghana. "My host family has set aside land for me so that when I marry my Ghanaian husband, there will be a place for me," she reports.

Program staff say that, in spite of the best efforts to ensure a positive student-host family situation, mismatches can occur. Depending on the nature of the problem, staff may intervene and, in some cases, a family (most often on the recommendation of the program) arranges to have a student return home. Time-off consultants advise that often a negative experience can be due to unrealistic expectations and incomplete research on the part of the student—yet another reason to do the up-front work to be aware of what your child is getting into!

What You Can Do

- Help your student understand the pros and cons of homestays and host families
- If there are bumps in the early part of the road, recognize this is not unusual
- Realize that strong bonds and even the realization of a "second family" can result from homestays

FOOD

"My host mother in Ghana was a 'dried fish' person," Laurel Wamsley recalls, recounting the role food played during her time abroad. "That is, she would go to the Volta Lake once a week and get lots of dried fish to sell. [The] best meals would be like peanut soup, kind of like ground nut soup, with rice balls, (kind of like Spanish rice). I'm not used to eating like that. . . .

Ghana is a carb-intensive society. So my host mother started making salad and chicken that I *could* eat."

For Mitchell Levene in Costa Rica, the first major breakthough with his host mother was with food. "At first, I ate everything in front of me, because I didn't want to offend my host mother," he says. His homestay mom was wise to what he was up to because he was eating everything and didn't notice that the other kids didn't clean their plates.

"One day she cooked ceviche," recalls Mitchell. The native delicacy of marinated raw fish wasn't in his culinary comfort zone. "I finally said that I was sorry, but that I couldn't eat it. It was hard for me to get it out . . . but she looked so relieved, and that was our breakthrough."

Adam's time-off experience included learning to grow and cook his own food in New Zealand and dining with his host family in Costa Rica. His experiences had a lasting impact on his view of food and its cultural importance as well as his eating habits.

"Food is a part of time off that teaches culture and health, and through which you can learn about the people you are sharing a meal with. I ate fast food like it was my job all through high school. I never even considered what it did to my body or to the environment. I didn't know how to cook (do pasta, oatmeal, or cereal count?) and had no desire to learn. What's the point of cooking when you can run to a fast-food restaurant and pick up a forty-cent cheeseburger? Now I wouldn't touch fast food with a ten-foot, burned French fry.

"In Costa Rica I didn't eat one meal of fast food. It was rice, beans, eggs from my backyard, cows from my backyard, and yes, one time I tried armadillo. Never again will I eat something that people describe as 'something we found dead on the farm.' Rice and beans for every meal has become second nature to me, and I've learned to love it. Other, that is, than the first week of digestive adjusting. My advice is to take some Metamucil if you ever go to Central America.

"New Zealand taught me to cook and eat healthily, showing me the advantages as well as the sustainability of vegetarianism. I am now able to cook for myself whenever I want to as well as know that I'm not contributing to the fast-food nation."

What You Can Do

- Research the foods, cuisine, and any dietary challenges related to the state, region, or country your student is traveling to (particularly if the program does not cover the topic of food in its orientation)
- Ensure that your student takes along any digestive medicine (if appropriate)
- When the student returns home, ask for anecdotes related to food and meals—they can be a great conversation starter and reveal much more than what was eaten from a plate

READJUSTING

We shouldn't have been surprised about the strong reactions we heard from students about the challenges posed by returning home from a gap experience and figuring out how to assimilate and bridge their "new present" to the past. The distance they can feel from friends and American society and the yearning to be understood in light of what they have been through is compelling and worth listening to.

"The irony was that coming back home was so foreign,"

one time-off veteran said. This is a sentiment shared by other gappers.

"No one can understand," David Miller explained. "I can try to share, but I'm the only one who's lived this year and lived my life. I'm in a much different place than I was a year ago."

"You don't come back without culture shock." That was the conclusion of Jordan Price, whose time-off journeys took him to Southeast Asia. "Coming back from Thailand and fitting back in was really hard after a mind-changing experience. Nobody wanted to sit and listen to me talk about Thailand, although coming back from Vietnam was better. My host family in Vietnam has e-mail—which is awesome! It's hard to find people who can relate—you try to explain what profound experiences you've been through and friends say, 'That's great . . . Want to go see a movie?'"

"I got asked questions about little details over and over again, like 'How did you deal without electricity and water?'" Laurel Wamsley said on returning from Africa. "But people didn't ask about the big picture."

"It was tougher coming home than going. Being home was really, really overwhelming," was Mitchell Levene's experience on returning to Texas. "I realized that when I was down in Costa Rica, I opened myself to everything around me. Returning to the United States, there was such a comparative sensory overload." Mitchell recalled visiting a mall a few days after he returned to Dallas and "walking in and starting to feel dizzy and claustrophobic. The music and lights . . . it was overwhelming."

Adam concurred with his peers. "Coming back is definitely the hardest part of time off. The more people you talk to who have the experience, the more you realize how common it is. For me, coming back from New Zealand was the hardest because I was 'still in the woods' as one former teacher put it. I had lived sustainably and contributed to nature for three months, not to mention working at a Buddhist retreat. I wasn't the same person when I came back. People would ask me, 'How was New Zealand?' I would say, 'Awesome.' I thought almost every time I was asked this question, 'Do you really want to know who I am now and why I am that way? . . . Do you want me to tell you about the things I've seen this year and the things I've discovered about myself . . . or do you want me to just say, 'It was cool'?

"I wanted more people to be interested in what I had done and the people I had met and loved, the evolution of my values, the evolution of my heart. I wanted people to care about the new Adam and embrace him. I didn't find those people. Don't get me wrong, there were those who really did want to know, but not as many as I had hoped. This 'coming down' was almost as important to me as the experiences themselves. I have developed more from those times than I could have ever imagined."

Adam's yearning to connect his new Costa Rican world with his United States home included encouraging his mother to return with him to the village where he had spent ten weeks teaching and bonding with new faces and a new culture.

Her story is an example of how time off can lead to expanded horizons, not only for students, but also for their parents.

"I always get the best sense of what my children are doing when I can see them in the environment they're in, especially when they're away from home," Wrenna said of her decision to travel with Adam back to his Costa Rican village. "When he was back in the United States, around Christmas, Adam said, 'You have to go!' and I looked into it and decided I could."

Wrenna, an elementary schoolteacher, designed lesson plans and carefully selected books and other educational materials to share with the fourth- and sixth-graders that she would co-teach with her son in Costa Rica. "I hadn't studied Spanish since high school, but I listened to language tapes," Wrenna recalled.

"They really value children in Costa Rica," she observed. "There is a lot of play and hugging and verbal as well as nonverbal communication." Some communication vehicles are universal, however. Wrenna found children reading *Harry Potter* and watching *The Karate Kid* on television.

One memorable moment occurred during a presentation ceremony at the village elementary school. ("There were three ceremonies in three days—these are incredibly hospitable people," Wrenna recalled). First, the students walked in with the Costa Rican flag followed by others carrying the American flag. Then a recording of the Costa Rican national anthem was played as the students sang along. "Then Adam and I were expected to sing the American national anthem—a capella," Wrenna said.

Wrenna was also on hand when the local school unveiled a library that was named after Adam and one of his U.S. partners. As a special project for the community that is part of the Global Routes program, they had raised funds to buy books for the "school that had nothing but is rich because the kids want to learn."

When asked about Adam's experiences today, Wrenna says, "Adam took time off because he felt a need to serve, and he did so in a purposeful way. It took courage for him to do what he did."

What You Can Do

- Give the student some space and time to process what he or she has been through

- Let the child share pictures and talk about experiences—and, while hearing the stories, listen to what is said between the lines
- When home, don't be surprised if your child spends time contacting peers or a host family from his time-off experience (and is less interested in spending time with some former friends or in activities that may now seem trivial)
- Take the time to learn more about where your child has returned from—even consider venturing there yourself or with other family members

7

Life Beyond Time Off

For life is a kind of handicraft that must be learned thoroughly and industriously, and diligently practiced, if we are not to have mere butchers and babblers as the issue of it all!
—*FRIEDRICH NIETZSCHE*

ONE OF THE UNANTICIPATED joys of researching this book was unearthing the stories of time-off pioneers—adults who, with the luxury and validation of time, shared their stories from years ago of taking a break from the formal education track. Their perspective and advice are an inspiration and provide a legacy for current and future time-off generations.

Cary Milner never wanted to go straight to college. Her sentiments were reminiscent of those heard from today's time-off students. In the 1990s she wanted "to be in a completely different place and out of my comfort zone." She had discovered a book on Mother Teresa's life and work, and, after absorbing it, she "knew that was where she wanted to spend her time." She applied and deferred entrance to college, went to work, and saved money for a plane ticket to India.

Her experiences there indeed carried her far outside her comfort zone, in ways that most Americans couldn't even imagine.

She spent two months working for the Kalighat House in Calcutta, tending to the sick and dying. She estimates that roughly half of the people in her care died while she was there. Then she spent a month trekking in Nepal, where she faced her own medical challenge. "I was in four wrecks while overseas where I wasn't hurt, but then I became really ill in Nepal due to bad water. I had to be airlifted out from where I was trekking in Katmandu." She credits "being around friends who cared about her" with helping her through the critical situation.

In retrospect, Cary Milner considers that many experiences during her time off "challenged her limits" and those of her peers. While in India, she recalls, "One day a nun came in and asked a group of us, 'Who here has administered shots?' A friend from Australia said jokingly, 'I've given shots to my horses back home.' The nun said, 'That's fine. There are two hundred people who need your help.' This type of situation was a common occurrence during my time there."

Like many students today, there was reverse culture shock when she returned to the United States. "A note to parents—help your child when he or she is at loose ends because it is extremely hard to readjust, and he or she needs your help in transitioning to the world he or she knew," says Cary.

In adjusting to college, "it was hard to relate to, especially because I wasn't partying with the rest of the freshmen. I had to find my own niche—people who were more mature and thinking in more worldly terms."

Cary's time off changed her perspective on college because "I realized how lucky students are in the United States to have the chance to be exposed to higher education." Today, Cary says, she "always values what I have that others in the world don't—a house and food, and I don't have to worry about starving to death."

She offers this practical advice for today's parents: "Encourage your kids to take time off because it makes life easier on the parents! Your child gets to learn that they shouldn't take things for granted, grows to be more responsible, and can even learn to do the dishes."

Kathy Olson, who today is vice president for education, job and life skills at the United Way of the Midlands in Columbia, South Carolina, wasn't sure what she wanted to do after graduating from high school in Iowa. Then her sister and brother-in-law, who were stationed in Italy at the time, offered an invitation that would change her life. "You belong on a college campus, but you're struggling right now with what direction to take," she recalls their saying during one conversation. "Maybe some time in a different landscape would be good for you." They proposed to buy her a plane ticket to Europe as long as she agreed to stay abroad for at least a year. "About six months after high school graduation, I jumped on a plane!"

"People and experiences opened doors and my mind in ways that going to school never would have," says Kathy. Once overseas, she traveled throughout Europe and visited museums. She recalls an opportunity to see Michelangelo's *David* in person. "I peeked through the wooden doors of the museum and saw an eighteen-foot sculpture instead of the miniature I imagined from pictures in art books. Everything was bigger than life!"

A friend "who was inspired by my energy and enthusiasm" got Kathy into a University of Maryland program that allowed her to take art classes in Italy with a professor who was "*the* English-speaking authority on Venetian art." She also did volunteer work in military schools, and that led to the contributions she makes as a nonprofit executive today.

"There I was, from landlocked Iowa, with the opportunity to see the world!"

She admits to a couple of questionable situations, for example, when a driver tried to steal her passport and when a friend got a piece of metal in her eye and they had to navigate health-care systems.

Kathy believes that "when you look at the statistics of how many students drop out that first year of college, there should be alternatives to going straight from high school to further formal education."

Her advice to today's students who are considering a time-off option: "Go for it. You'll love it! The world is a little different now, and you'll probably need a more structured adventure, so do your research. Prepare yourself, and don't let anything stand in your way."

David Neidorf, director of the Integrated Studies Program at Middlebury College, says of his time off that "what changed me was having real responsibility."

His journey began with the realization during his early years at a selective liberal arts college that he "wasn't living up to his self-defined potential." David took a break to channel an abundance of spirited energy into Outward Bound as well as search-and-rescue pursuits. He discovered that when immersed in these experiences, he was able to focus on "who I *am* and *could be* instead of the challenges of school."

When he returned to college "he was there because he was interested" and pursued studies in philosophy and music. Today, at Middlebury College, he is able to teach representatives from the current generation of time-off students. When asked to name the most powerful influences in his life, he cites, along with his wife and children, "my parents and the wilderness that taking time off helped me discover."

He would recommend that other students—and even his

own children—consider taking time off from the formal education track.

Cary, Kathy, and David are among the pioneers whose stories continue to inform and inspire current and future time-off achievers.

One last thought: There is no graduation speech when our children leave for their time-off experiences. Partings at airports, bus and train stations, and in driveways are opportunities for parents to offer what is most on their minds and in their hearts.

What came to us as Adam began his gap experiences was that now it was the world that would embrace him. And supporting him as he left to find his destiny and who he will become was, is, and will be our greatest gift of graduation.

PART 2

Programs and Resources

Programs and Resources Overview

In this section, you'll find information on some of the many programs available to students and parents researching gap-year options. We've divided them into sections that cover:

- Community service and volunteering
- Studying
- Exploring and traveling
- Working and interning

We have focused on reputable programs that have solid attributes and are geared toward or include a dedication to individuals aged eighteen through twenty-four. Where appropriate, we've included a program in more than one section. Additional Web sites included in the program section feature searchable databases or provide other information that may be useful.

Although every attempt has been made to be accurate and

current in descriptions, locations, costs, and other areas (in many cases, we contacted program staff for information or had them review their entry), much of the information is based on the most recent content available on the programs' Web sites. *Please take the time to check Web sites for the most up-to-date information, including current costs and program offerings and locations.*

We've also included resource information on:
- Consultants and counseling services
- Travel and housing
- Fund-raising
- Health and safety

Again, we have sought to provide the most up-to-date and accurate information, but be sure to check with the appropriate Web site or call the organization directly.

I. PROGRAMS

Community Service and Volunteering—United States

By the time they graduate from high school, most students have participated in community service or other volunteer activities. Building on these familiar skills through a structured program over a period of time allows them to develop an appreciation for regions and subcultures of the United States and gain the satisfaction of "giving back." Programs that focus on domestic community service can be less expensive than their international counterparts and entail less complex travel arrangements and fewer credentials (e.g., no passports or visas). Students participating in the programs in this area can be compensated in some way (stipend, educational award, room and board, etc.) or they can serve as unpaid volunteers.

American Red Cross
www.redcross.org
2025 E Street, NW

Washington, DC 20006
Phone: 202-303-4498

Description: The American Red Cross, a humanitarian organization led by volunteers and is guided by its congressional charter and the fundamental principles of the International Red Cross movement to provide relief to victims of disasters and help people prevent, prepare for, and respond to emergencies.

The Red Cross is one of the largest and most easily recognized volunteer organizations in the world. It offers a great program for students looking for volunteer opportunities near their homes or in communities around the United States. For students interested in the medical field, Red Cross experience can provide an ideal introduction to a career. The Web site has a search tool that describes positions in local communities.

Locations: Check out the Web site, which has more than 100 places for volunteers in the United States.

Supervision: Varied. The Red Cross covers a wide range of volunteer jobs, and training for them is usually a must, so it is felt that volunteers should have someone looking after them who is responsible.

Costs/Compensation: These are volunteer positions. Contact specific location through Web site for details

AmeriCorps
www.americorps.org
1201 New York Avenue, NW
Washington, DC 20525
Phone: 202-606-5000

Description: AmeriCorps is a network of national service programs engaging more than 50,000 Americans each year to meet critical needs in areas of education, public safety, health, and the environment. AmeriCorps members serve through more than 2,100 nonprofits, public agencies, and faith-based organizations. They tutor and mentor youth, build affordable housing, teach computer skills, clean parks and streams, run after-school programs, and help communities respond to disasters. A scientific study of AmeriCorps' long-term effects reveals "a powerful positive impact on members' attitudes and behaviors in areas of civic engagement, education, employment and life skills." AmeriCorps was founded with four main goals.

1. *Getting Things Done.* AmeriCorps members help communities solve problems in the areas of education, public safety, the environment, and other human needs (like health and housing) by serving directly and by getting other people to serve as volunteers.

2. *Strengthening Communities.* AmeriCorps members help unite individuals from all different backgrounds—and organizations of all kinds—in a common effort to improve communities.

3. *Encouraging Responsibility.* AmeriCorps members explore and exercise their responsibilities to their communities, their families, and themselves—during their service experience and throughout their lives.

4. *Expanding Opportunity.* AmeriCorps helps those who help America. AmeriCorps members receive awards to further their education or to pay back student loans. They also gain valuable job experience, specialized training, and other skills.

AmeriCorps encourages citizen service by funding a smorgasbord of local nonprofits focused on community service. A prospective AmeriCorps member can choose any of the 2,100 AmeriCorps funded programs and apply to any of them or more than one.

Locations: Anywhere in the United States, American Samoa, and Puerto Rico.

Supervision: Low. Your child likely will be responsible for himself or herself during his or her volunteer service.

Costs/Compensation: Paid positions. AmeriCorps members are eligible for a $4,725 education award after successfully completing a term of service. The term of service is ten months to a year, during which the member is required to complete 1,700 hours of service in order to graduate and receive the education award. While a parent might choose to supplement the child's income, this probably won't be necessary. The most a parent should expect to pay is the first and last months' rent, if housing is not provided. AmeriCorps members are eligible for basic health care coverage.

City Year
www.cityyear.org
285 Columbus Avenue
Boston, MA 02116
Phone: 617-927-2500

Description: An "action tank" for national service, City Year seeks to demonstrate, improve, and promote the concept of national service as a means of building a stronger democracy. City Year's vision is that, one day, the question most commonly asked of an eighteen-year-old will be: "Where are you going to do your service year?"

Each day, at fifteen sites across the country, a thousand City Year members put on their boots and join up to work in schools, after-school programs, and other programs designed to meet

critical needs in the community. In each city the group of City Year members is known as the "corps." The different corps, which range in size from 30 to 200 individuals, are divided into diverse teams of about ten members each. Within a few weeks these teams—comprising people of various ages, religions, sexual orientations, race, and heritage—are working together. The program, in which all corps members are required to wear a uniform provided by the Timberland Company, is designed to break down social barriers and to erase racism, sexism, ageism, and bigotry, first from within the corps and then within the community. *Locations:* City Year has programs across the country, in such cities as Boston, Chicago, Cleveland, Columbia, SC, Columbus, Detroit, Little Rock, New York, Philadelphia, Rhode Island, San Antonio, San Jose, Seattle, and Washington, DC.
Supervision: Low. Expect your child to be responsible for himself or herself.
Costs/Compensation: Full-time members receive living stipends and health insurance coverage. Upon successful completion (a minimum of 1700 hours) members are eligible for a $4,725 education award.

Habitat for Humanity International
www.habitat.org
E-mail: publicinfo@hfhi.org
Partner Service Center
121 Habitat Street
Americus, GA 31709-3498
Phone: 229-924-6935, ext. 2551 or 2552

Habitat invites people of all backgrounds, races, and religions to build houses together in partnership with families in need of shelter.

Description: Habitat for Humanity International is a nonprofit, ecumenical Christian housing ministry. Founded in 1976 by Millard Fuller and his wife, Linda, HFHI seeks to·eliminate poverty and homelessness from the world and to make decent shelter a matter of conscience and action. Local Habitat affiliates coordinate house building and select partner families.

Locations: Habitat for Humanity has salaried, hourly, and stipend volunteer positions available at their international headquarters in Americus, Georgia, and at field locations around the world and in the United States. The international arm of Habitat runs youth programs in Africa, the Middle East, Asia and the Pacific, Europe, Central Asia, Latin America, and the Caribbean.

Supervision: Contact Habitat for details.

Costs/Compensation: Primarily volunteer positions. An Ameri-Corps option is available with members eligible for a living stipend (up to $9,900 for 11 months), health insurance, and a $4,725 education award.

Public Allies

www.publicallies.org
633 W. Wisconsin Avenue, Suite 610
Milwaukee, WI 53203
Phone: 414-273-0533

Description: Public Allies envisions communities where people of different backgrounds, beliefs, and experiences work together and share responsibility for improving their own lives and the lives of those around them. Public Allies advances diverse young leaders to strengthen communities, nonprofits, and civic participation.

Public Allies "identifies talented young adults from diverse backgrounds and advances their leadership through a ten-month program of full-time, paid apprenticeships in nonprofit organizations, weekly leadership trainings, and team service projects." The focus of the Public Allies program is the development of leadership not service. Public Allies believes that program alumni, through the exposure and training afforded to them, will do the most good by becoming future leaders in the nonprofit sector and in the community.

Locations: Bridgeport, Hartford, and New Haven, CT; Chicago, IL; Cincinnati, OH; Estes Park, CO; Los Angeles, CA; Milwaukee, WI; New York, NY; Raleigh-Durham, NC; Silicon Valley, CA; and Wilmington, DE.

Supervision: Purposely low. The development of leadership requires personal responsibility.

Costs/Compensation: These are volunteer positions. Contact a specific location through Web site for details.

The Student Conservation Association
www.thesca.org
689 River Road
P.O. Box 550
Charlestown, NH 03603-0550
Phone: 603-543-1700

Description: The Student Conservation Association is the "nation's leading provider of conservation service opportunities, outdoor skills, and leadership training" for youth. Volunteer opportunities are available in the nation's parks and forests, historic and cultural resources, and urban green spaces. From the Web site's Parents' Page: "Allowing a loved one to travel far from home to an often unfamiliar environment is not a decision to be taken lightly. But it can also result in an unforgettable, transformational, once-in-a-lifetime experience that will positively impact your child for years and years to come."

Locations: Opportunities through programs in all fifty states.

Supervision: Participants are supervised by program staff.

Costs/Compensation: Conservation internships in the Conservation Corps are open on a competitive basis to individuals eighteen years of age and older. Expenses are paid, and a "living allowance" of $50-$300 per week may be provided, along with a travel grant.

World Volunteer Web

www.worldvolunteerweb.org

Description: "The WorldVolunteerWeb.org supports the volunteer community by providing a global one-stop shop for information, resources, and organizations linked to volunteerism. It aims to represent the diversity of volunteerism in all of its cultural forms, bringing global ideals to local voluntary actions. Coordinated by the United Nations Volunteer program, it mobilizes individuals, organizations, and networks to help achieve the Millennium Development Goals (MDGs), a set of time-bound targets to combat poverty, hunger, disease, illiteracy, environmental degradation, and discrimination against women. To promote ties between civil society organizations, governments, and individual volunteers, the MDGs feature prominently in WorldVolunteerWeb.org."

The site offers vast resources about volunteering in the United States and around the world.

Costs/Compensation: Free.

Community Service and
Volunteering—International

For students who want to travel abroad, get out of their comfort zone, learn about another culture or language, and give back through service, community service or volunteer work overseas is a good option. If a student has not traveled internationally, many recommend choosing a program with considerable structure and staff support. Through participation in international service, students learn to travel independently and navigate in different regions of the world while having the satisfaction of addressing a real need in the areas of education, the environment, health care, or other aspects of individual, community, or economic development. The programs below offer opportunities on most continents and some include a homestay with a host family. Most of them have fees, and travel abroad may be included in that fee.

GENERAL SITES

International Volunteer Programs Association
www.volunteerinternational.org
IVPA
P.O. Box 18
Presque Isle, MI 49777
Phone: 989-595-3667

Description: A great Web site and organization for helping the student decide where to volunteer. It offers a search engine that searches the world over for programs you are interested in. The organization is affiliated with more than thirty volunteering organizations, including AFS and the International Volunteer Program, among many others.
Costs: Free.

World Volunteer Web
www.worldvolunteerweb.org
(See page 134 for a full description)
Costs: Free.

SPECIFIC SITES

AFS Intercultural Programs, Inc.
www.afs.org
E-mail: info.center@afs.org
71 West 23rd Street, 17th Floor
New York, NY 10010
Phone: 212-807-8686

AFS has offices in fifty countries and recommends contacting respective country offices (see Web site for details).

Description: Engaged in international exchange since 1919, AFS is a "leader in intercultural learning and offers exchange programs in more than fifty countries around the world through independent, not-for-profit AFS organizations, each with a network of volunteers, a professionally staffed office, and headed up by a volunteer board. AFS International provides worldwide leadership, coordination, support, quality control, and development of AFS organizations and programs." AFS offers school-year and summer programs for high school students and community-based volunteer programs for individuals eighteen years of age and older. Placements range from four months to a year.

Locations: Africa, Asia, Europe, Latin America, and North America.

Supervision: Depends on location and program.

Costs/Compensation: Stipends and fees vary based on the program.

Alliance Abroad Group

www.allianceabroad.com
1221 South Mopac Expressway, Suite 250
Austin, TX 78746
Phone: 512-457-8062
Toll-free: 1-888-6-ABROAD

Description: The "spirit" of Alliance Abroad is based on four principles: "(1) the life principle, especially in man, originally regarded as inherent in the breath or as infused by a deity, (2) the thinking, motivating, feeling part, (3) a divine animating influence or inspiration, (4) vivacity, courage, vigor, enthusiasm."

Alliance Abroad offers international programs designed to match a variety of interests. It offers volunteer positions, language studies, work abroad, and teaching placements. Alliance Abroad experiences include living with a host family while volunteering and learning a language.

Locations: Argentina, Australia, China, Costa Rica, Ecuador, England, Greece, Hawaii, Mexico, Peru, South Africa, and Spain.

Supervision: Moderate. In-country support at all times, in-country pickup, and local orientation.

Costs/Compensation: Program fees vary, based on type and location.

AmeriSpan
www.amerispan.com
E-mail: info@amerispan.com
P.O. Box 58129
Philadelphia, PA 19102-8129
Phone: 215-751-1100
Toll-free: 1-800-879-6640

Description: Through AmeriSpan, a student can study abroad, intern abroad, study a new language, and travel, or you can choose to participate in one of their specialized programs for health professionals, teachers, or international businessmen and women. Drawing on its experience with thousands of clients, AmeriSpan knows the ins and outs of international cultural exchange, and it is very confident that it has a high level of customer support.

"AmeriSpan was created in 1993 by and for lovers of language, travel, and cultures. Starting as a two-person operation with a passion for Latin America, we have grown to be one of the leaders in educational travel with over 20,000 past clients.

We started out as specialists in Latin America and have since applied our expertise to many other languages and regions. Collectively, our staff has traveled to more than sixty-five countries—every continent except Antarctica—and speaks ten languages. We offer a variety of educational travel programs, including language programs and volunteer and internship placements."

Locations: These programs are located in Africa, Asia, Europe, the Middle East, and South and Central America.

Supervision: Varied. AmeriSpan has a wide range of programs; some offer plenty of supervision, while others offer none, other than that in its international support system.

Costs: Four weeks at a language school in a foreign country cost about $700 and up.

Amigos de las Américas
www.amigoslink.org
E-mail: info@amigoslink.org
5618 Star Lane
Houston, TX 77057
Phone: 713-782-5290
Toll-free: 1-800-231-7796

Description: Amigos de las Américas builds partnerships to empower young leaders, advance community development, and strengthen multicultural understanding in the Americas. Amigos works with small community-based organizations in many Latin American and Caribbean countries in the fields of education, conservation, and health care. Programs generally last five to eight weeks during the summer months and can range from working in hospitals throughout Costa Rica to running a day camp in the Dominican Republic.

Locations: Brazil, Costa Rica, the Dominican Republic, Honduras, Mexico, Nicaragua, Panama, and Paraguay.

Supervision: High. A project leader is present for the entire process, but Amigos is a strong believer in the fact that volunteers can start to take on more responsibility if they feel capable.

Costs: The cost of the program is $3,625 and includes international round-trip airfare from Miami or Houston.

Blue Ventures
www.blueventures.org
E-mail: volunteer@blueventures.org
52 Avenue Road
London N6 5DR
United Kingdom
Phone: 011-44-20-8341-9819 from U.S.

Description: For those fishy people out there who want to spend their time off in a beautiful tropical environment while doing extensive diving and research projects. Blue Ventures includes dive certification in its fee, but does not include the wet suit and diving accessories. Volunteers will work hand-in-hand with local biologists, marine institutes, NGOs, and communities whose livelihoods depend on marine ecosystems.

Locations: The Comoros Islands, Madagascar, New Zealand, South Africa, and Tanzania.

Supervision: High. Volunteers live with their supervisors and fellow workers.

Costs: For six-week placements, the cost is $3,100, which includes dive certification and scientific research training. Remember: the wet suit and goggles are not included. A volunteer can stay for another six-week term at a lower price of about $2,100.

Cross-Cultural Solutions

www.crossculturalsolutions.org
E-mail: info@crossculturalsolutions.org
2 Clinton Place
New Rochelle, NY 10801
Phone: 914-632-0022
Toll-free: 1-800-380-4777

Description: Cross-Cultural Solutions operates volunteer programs around the world in partnership with sustainable community initiatives, bringing people together to work side-by-side while sharing perspectives and fostering cultural understanding.

A participant's interests are assessed by the organization, and then he or she is placed in one of many local affiliated programs. There are opportunities for educating children and adults, as well as caring for infants and the elderly, and working with medical staff on many projects (such as caring for HIV/AIDS patients). Most programs run from two to twelve weeks. These programs also include excursions to nearby points of interest, special events, and discussions with a variety of local cultural representatives, professionals, and community agencies.

Locations: Brazil, China, Costa Rica, Ghana, Guatemala, India, Peru, Russia, Tanzania, and Thailand.

Supervision: Moderate. In-country staff address any problems that may arise and help cross-cultural interaction. There is also a toll-free twenty-four-hour emergency hot line.

Costs: Average costs for two-week programs are $2,175; twelve-week programs are $4,655. The program fee also covers health and travel insurance. The Web site states that "all program fees and the cost of international airfare are U.S. tax-deductible."

Doctors Without Borders
www.doctorswithoutborders.org
E-mail: through Web site
333 Seventh Avenue, 2nd Floor
New York, NY 10001-5004
Phone: 212-679-6800

Description: Doctors Without Borders delivers emergency aid to victims of armed conflict, epidemics, and natural and man-made disasters, and to others who lack health care due to social or geographical isolation.

A program for those looking to work in areas that may not be considered the safest in the world, Doctors Without Borders is an organization that goes where most people and professionals aren't willing to go because of a crisis. They work on AIDS projects, have massive vaccination campaigns, train local doctors in crisis areas, improve water sanitation, and feed starving populations, among other projects. They accept office volunteers with little to no experience but have strict selection criteria for "in the field" volunteers, such as two years of professional experience.

Locations: According to the Web site, Doctors Without Borders will go anywhere that has wars and conflicts, refugees and displaced people, natural and man-made disasters, any place, in fact, that needs long-term assistance. Office volunteers can work in New York or Los Angeles.

Supervision: Expect little. This is more of a program for responsible individuals who want to help in areas having the greatest need.

Costs: The volunteer is expected to pay his or her own costs, which vary depending on the destination.

Global Citizens Network
www.globalcitizens.org
E-mail: info@globalcitizens.org
130 N. Howell Street
St. Paul, MN 55104
Phone: 651-644-0960
Toll-free: 1-800-644-9292

Description: The mission of Global Citizens Network is to create "a network of people who are committed to the shared values of peace, justice, tolerance, cross-cultural understanding, and global cooperation; to the preservation of indigenous cultures, traditions, and ecologies; and to the enhancement of the quality of life around the world."

"Volunteers assist community people working on locally initiated projects, providing the human resources of mental and physical labor while working under the leadership of community people. Each team visits a developing community where local people are involved in grassroots efforts to meet their human and community needs while preserving their culture and traditions. Volunteers are instructed in language, social structure and issues, agriculture, industry, and arts."

Locations: Arizona, New Mexico, Washington, Guatemala, Kenya, Mexico, Nepal, and Tanzania.

Supervision: High. Supervised by a local organization as well as a team leader who accompanies the group.

Costs: The program cost of $650–$1,950 covers in-country travel and lodging, most meals, orientation materials, a share of the team leader's expenses (team leaders are not paid), and a donation to the village project for one- to three-week trips.

Global Crossroad

www.globalcrossroad.com
E-mail: info@globalcrossroad.com
8738 Quarters Lake Road
Baton Rouge, LA 70809
Phone: 225-922-7854
Toll-free: 1-800-413-2008

Description: Global Crossroad supports grassroots projects that offer hope to the rural poor in developing countries, especially orphans and women, and offer the challenges of the developing countries to volunteers. "We also hope to offer a unique opportunity of cultural immersion to international volunteers through a uniquely designed language program, cultural visits, and village visits in many countries. Our last aim is to offer an alternative way of traveling or travel learning to international volunteers through our mini-adventure projects."

Program offerings include teaching, mini-adventures (ecotourism through multiple countries), language study, and internships in many countries. Global Crossroad offers two programs based in China and Thailand that are free for volunteer teachers. Volunteer programs usually run from four to twenty-four weeks and the teaching programs run from two to fifty-two weeks.

Locations: China, Costa Rica, Ecuador, Ghana, India, Kenya, Mongolia, Nepal, Sri Lanka, and Thailand.

Supervision: Moderate to high. Local coordinators are stationed in each project area. They help to orient the volunteer and run a language program for two weeks, then check in on the participant every one to four weeks.

Costs: Very reasonable. Global Crossroad keeps costs to a minimum, so program fees range from free to about $1,800 for its twelve-week volunteer programs. Travel insurance and health insurance are provided with the program fee.

Global Routes
www.globalroutes.org
E-mail: mail@globalroutes.org
One Short Street
Northampton, MA 01060
Phone: 413-585-8895

Description: Global Routes, a tax-exempt nonprofit, is a nongovernmental, nonsectarian organization committed to strengthening the global community and fostering greater self-understanding through cross-cultural living and community service.

Since 1986 Global Routes has been offering experiential-based community service programs and teaching internships that allow high school and college-aged students to live and work with people in rural communities throughout the world. Homestays are an integral part of the Global Routes experience.
Locations: Include Belize, China, Costa Rica, the Dominican Republic, Ecuador, Ghana, Guadeloupe, Kenya, New Zealand, St. Lucia, Thailand, Vietnam, and the United States (depending on type of program).
Supervision: High. Group leaders facilitate travel, homestays, and volunteer projects for the duration of the volunteer's program.
Costs: Reasonably priced. Program fees reflect the high level of supervision and extra travel and training components: one-month high school programs in the summer range from $3,750 to $5,350, not including airfare; three-month college programs are $4,300 to $4,600 not including airfare.

Global Service Corps
www.globalservicecorps.org
E-mail: gsc@earthisland.org
300 Broadway, Suite 28
San Francisco, CA 94133-3312
Phone: 415-788-3666 x128

Description: Global Service Corps (GSC) is a nonprofit international volunteer organization that provides volunteer opportunities for people worldwide to live and work abroad in developing countries, such as Thailand and Tanzania. Programs focus on needs in the areas of health, environment, education, and agriculture. Volunteers live with host families. Programs are either short-term (two to four weeks) or longer (six weeks to a year). An international internship runs from six to ten weeks. GSC is affiliated with the Earth Island Institute. Youth of college age are encouraged to apply.
Locations: Tanzania and Thailand.
Supervision: Moderate. In-country coordinators and host families provide assistance and support.
Costs: There are application and program fees of about $3,700 for a ten-week stay. "All program fees, including airfare, are tax deductible to the full extent of the law."

Global Vision International
www.gvi.co.uk
E-mail: info@gvi.co.uk
Amwell Farmhouse
Nomansland, Unit 10, Wheathampstead, St Albans
Herts, AL4 8EJ
United Kingdom
Phone: 011-44-870-608-8898

Description: "Global Vision International promotes sustainable solutions for a rapidly changing world by matching the general public with international environmentalists, researchers, and pioneering educators."

Global Vision's opportunities are divided into four different types: expeditions, projects, courses, and national parks. Each has exotic locations to choose from and huge varieties of experiences. GVI's main goals are working in conservation and providing humanitarian assistance throughout the world, with projects that make sure long-term actions will be taken in a certain area. Volunteers provide the workforce and financial backing for helping the world.

"Global Vision International was formed in 1998 to provide support and services to international charities, nonprofits, and governmental agencies. Through our international network of forty personnel in over twenty countries, GVI continues to support many of the most critical conservation and humanitarian projects around the globe.

"GVI is a nonpolitical, nonreligious organization, which, through its alliance with aid-reliant organizations throughout the world, provides opportunities to volunteers to fill a critical void in the fields of environmental research, conservation, education, and community development. To date over 1,500 volunteers have joined projects resulting in the direct financial support of over UK £500,000 / U.S. $750,000."

Locations: Over fifteen countries throughout the world, including Madagascar, Mexico, Peru, Thailand, Indonesia, and Spain.

Supervision: Moderate to high. In-country, full-time support field coordinators are there whenever need be and provide full emergency support.

Costs: Since there are so many options, prices vary widely. A five-week South African expedition starts at around $2,590; a project of working with Mayan poverty in Guatemala for four weeks starts at $1,535; an outdoor fourteen-day survival class in Utah costs $1,525; and working for a South African national park for a year is about $5,540. Costs do not include international airfare or travel insurance.

Global Volunteers Network
www.volunteer.org.nz
E-mail: info@volunteer.org.nz
P.O. Box 2231
Wellington, New Zealand
Toll-free: 1-800-963-1198

Description: The organization supports the work of local community organizations in developing countries through the placement of international volunteers. "We believe that local communities are in the best position to determine their needs, and we provide volunteers to help them achieve their goals."

Each country in the network has different options; therefore it is hard to generalize opportunities. Volunteers can choose from experiences such as working at a Liberian refugee camp in Ghana, teaching English in China, or working with animals in Thailand.
Locations: Alaska, China, Ecuador, Ghana, Nepal, New Zealand, Romania, Russia, Thailand, Uganda, and Vietnam.
Supervision: Varied. Check out the Web site for programs of interest.
Costs: Prices vary depending on country. Teaching in Ghana costs $1,300 for six months, while conservation volunteerism in New Zealand costs $2,400 for eight weeks. Costs do not include airfare, travel insurance, or personal expenses (e.g., bottled water, entertainment).

i-to-i
www.i-to-i.com
E-mail: support@i-to-i.com
190 East Ninth Avenue, Suite 350
Denver, CO 80203
Phone: 303-765-5325
Toll-free: 1-800-985-4864

Description: i-to-i offers over 450 programs in twenty-four countries in many different fields. Teaching English was the main goal of i-to-i when it began, but the organization has grown into the fields of conservation, building, and ecotourism, among other volunteer opportunities. i-to-i also offers TEFL (Teaching English as a Foreign Language) certification, which means that graduates are able to earn money in many countries.

"i-to-i is a global community of 130 devoted professionals, in three offices worldwide, and thousands of volunteers working together to bring international cultures eye to eye. This community never sleeps. At any point in the day, somebody, somewhere, is working on an i-to-i project or TEFL course."

Locations: Destinations include Australia, Bolivia, Brazil, China, Costa Rica, Croatia, the Dominican Republic, Ecuador, Ghana, Guatemala, Honduras, India, Ireland, Kenya, Mexico, Mongolia, Nepal, Peru, South Africa, Sri Lanka, Tanzania, Thailand, and Vietnam.

Supervision: Moderate. In-country coordinators provide many services to the participant, including predeparture counseling on safety issues and arrival details, arrival pick-up, orientation to health and safety issues, arranged accommodation, and a twenty-four-hour pager system.

Costs: Programs start at around $1,200 for four weeks, and most run to about sixteen weeks with increases in price. See the Web site for more details about what the fees cover, such as comprehensive insurance.

The International Partnership
for Service-Learning and Leadership
www.ipsl.org
E-mail: info@ipsl.org
815 Second Avenue, Suite 315
New York, NY 10017
Phone: 212-986-0989

Description: IPS-L offers programs that unite academic study and volunteer service to the community in international and intercultural settings that are models for the practice of service-learning (where students develop through active participation in meaningful, organized activities that meet community needs) and promotes the theory and practice of service-learning through research, publications conferences, and training.

Its participants become a part of the area in which they live. "In many IPS-L programs students are housed with local families, thereby giving them another experience of and perspective on the society and culture. The IPS-L program directors arrange the homestays and know each family well. Most IPS-L families have hosted service-learning students year after year, some for as many as fifteen years."

Locations: Ecuador, the Czech Republic, England, France, India, Israel, Jamaica, Mexico, the Philippines, Russia, Scotland, South Dakota (Northern Plains Native Americans), and Thailand. See the Web site program matrix to get more information about each country and location.

Supervision: Moderate to high. IPS-L will help you get comfortable in your host location at first, then will set you free with the option of support from the IPS-L resident program director, service agency supervisor, the faculty and university support staff, the housing director, and, in most programs, the host family.

Costs: Costs are more than $7,000 a semester. Financial aid and scholarships from home institutions may be transferable to IPS-L programs, and credit transfer seems to be an integral part of the program, provided arrangements are made ahead of time.

International Volunteer Program
www.ivpsf.org
E-mail: layne@swiftusa.com
678 13th St., Suite 100
Oakland, CA 94612
Phone: 510-433-0414

Description: IVP offers "volunteer programs designed to facilitate hands-on service and international exchange opportunities and to foster cultural understanding at the local and global levels."

Founded in 1991, IVP provides volunteer staff for more than a hundred nonprofit organizations in Europe, the United States, and Latin America. Programs last six weeks and run during the summer. IVP was founded by the Société Française de Bienfaisance Mutuelle with the assistance of the French consulate in San Francisco, the University of California at Irvine, and the Comité des Jumelages de Troyes. Participants must be at least eighteen years old and have language skills (two years of college-level classes or the equivalent).

Locations: More than one hundred nonprofit organizations in Europe and the United States, as well as Costa Rica.

Supervision: Programs include twenty-four-hour, seven-day emergency contact and assistance service.

Costs: There is a program fee of $1,800 for every program except for Costa Rica, which costs $2,100—all for six-week programs. Comprehensive insurance is included in fees, along with in-country transportation, meals, and orientation.

Madventurer
www.madventurer.com
E-mail: team@madventurer.com
Hawthorn House
Forth Banks
Newcastle
NE1 3SG
United Kingdom
Phone: 011-44-845-121-1996 from U.S.

Description: Madventurer's goal is to assist rural community development while enabling adventurous travelers to gain experience through interaction with local people. This program is designed to combine hands-on volunteer work with adventure travel in Africa and South America.

"Madventurer combines award-winning development projects and adventurous overland travel to offer those taking a gap year, university students, and career-breakers a unique experience. You can join us for two weeks, five weeks, or three months on projects, and then undertake an adventure from three weeks to three months in duration."

Locations: Bolivia, Ghana, Kenya, Peru, Tanzania, Togo, Tonga, Trinidad, and Uganda.

Supervision: High. An in-country guide accompanies the participant throughout the program. First-aid support is available on site.

Costs: For a program that provides a long "adventure travel," expect to pay a bit more. Adventures can be selected, but they cost about $800 for three weeks, while program work starts at about $2,300 for a five-week stay and $3,350 for a three-month stay.

Operation Crossroads Africa
www.operationcrossroadsafrica.org
E-mail: oca@igc.org
P.O. Box 5570
New York, NY 10027
Phone: 212-289-1949

Description: Operation Crossroads Africa is an intercultural program that brings young westerners and Africans together to form strong relationships and make positive change in struggling communities. Founded in 1957, this organization has sent over 11,000 volunteers to Africa and Latin America. Volunteers work in education, construct buildings, and end up becoming part of a small rural community. This is a program with so much experience it has been called the "progenitor of the Peace Corps." A summer program runs for six weeks of service and is followed by a week of travel.
Locations: Seven to twelve African countries each summer as well as countries in Latin America.
Supervision: High. A group leader accompanies the group of eight to ten men and women for the duration of the program.
Costs: $3,500 seems pricey, international airfare from New York (which can cost upward of $1,500 to Africa) and health insurance are included in the fee.

Projects Abroad
www.projects-abroad.org
E-mail: info@projects-abroad.org

One Davol Square
Providence, RI 02903
Toll-free: 1-888-839-3535

Description: Started by a group of gappers in England in 1992 who were looking for a place to teach English, Projects Abroad has grown to include many options. Teaching is the main option, but not English only, as in most programs of this type. Participants can help teach another language, sports, drama, art, or the sciences. Programs also include conservation projects and animal care. Whether patrolling the beaches of Mexico for turtle nests or teaching biology in Ghana, these projects cover plenty of ground. Living with a host family is the common means of accommodation.

Projects Abroad also offers multiple-country teaching programs at a higher cost. See the Web site for more details.

Locations: Projects Abroad has nineteen countries in its network, including Australia, Chile, Germany, Ghana, Mexico, Nepal, and Peru.

Supervision: Moderate to high. A support base exists in every country with an in-country coordinator at the local office twenty-four hours a day, seven days a week. The in-country personnel also check in with the host families frequently to make sure everything is running smoothly with the volunteer.

Costs: Program fees vary by host country, starting at around $2,400 for a three-month stay, with an option to stay a month longer costing another $500 to $700. Medical insurance and travel insurance are covered in the fees as well.

Students Partnership Worldwide
www.spw.org
E-mail: spwuk@gn.apc.org

17 Dean's Yard
London SW1P 3PB
United Kingdom
Phone: 011-44-207-222-0138 from U.S.

Description: An invitation to "young people worldwide to play a lead role in tackling health and environmental threats in rural Africa and Asia," SPW works in rural communities with health and environmental programs for four-, six-, and eight-month volunteer placements. SPW volunteers should expect to be in the most desperate parts of the third world where AIDS patients and environmental degradation are in dire need of attention. Volunteers will assist in projects that will teach health and environmental education and where they can make significant contributions to the communities in which they are placed.

"Through community and school-based programs we work to empower young people, to help them get involved in the decisions that shape their future. In the deprived rural communities where SPW operates, the health services and the schools cannot provide the essential information and resources young people need to avoid life-threatening diseases like malaria and HIV/AIDS."

Locations: India, Nepal, South Africa, Tanzania, Uganda, Zambia, and Zimbabwe.

Supervision: Moderate. In-country support staff visit the participant two or three times during a placement and the organizations with which the volunteer works are carefully selected so that they will provide support as well.

Costs: For a six- to eight-month program, the price includes return flight and comprehensive insurance and averages about $5,300. (Program costs are calculated in pounds sterling, so they will be influenced by the exchange rate.)

VentureCo Worldwide
www.ventureco-worldwide.com
E-mail: mail@ventureco-worldwide.com
The Ironyard
64-66 The Market Place
Warwick CV34 4SD
United Kingdom
Phone: 011-44-192-641-1122 from U.S.

Description: VentureCo Worldwide offers sixteen-week gap-year programs and includes three different phases if you go to a country where the language is not your own. In South American or Central American programs, the participant starts with a three-week Spanish course. After the course and some orientation to the cultural background of the area, participants work on aid projects that can include conservation, building, or helping out a community in any way. A main part of VentureCo is the adventure attached to the end of the program, which is best suited to trekkers and adventurers.

Locations: These programs are generally multinational, but the names of the programs are Aztec-Maya, Inca, Himalayan, Patagonia, and Rift Valley.

Supervision: High. A group leader accompanies participants throughout the journey.

Costs: These programs involve a fair amount of travel and last for sixteen weeks and cost around $7,200. "The price . . . is all-inclusive and covers the cost of international flights, airport taxes, travel insurance, food, accommodation, language tuition, cultural orientation, expedition activities, and transport throughout the sixteen-week venture."

Volunteers for Peace
www.vfp.org
E-mail: vfp@vfp.org
1034 Tiffany Road
Belmont, Vermont 05730
Phone: 802-259-2759

Description: VFP promotes international voluntary service as an effective means of intercultural education and community service. VFP provides programs in which people from diverse backgrounds work together to help overcome violence and environmental decay.

VFP offers over 2,400 short-term voluntary service projects in over ninety countries, including three in Palestine. These international workcamps are an opportunity to complete meaningful community service while living and interacting in an intercultural environment. Work projects include: construction and renovation of low-income housing or community buildings, historic preservation, and archaeology; environmental projects such as trail building, environmental education, wildlife surveying, park maintenance, and organic farming; social services such as working with children, the elderly, the physically or mentally handicapped, refugees, minority groups, drug and alcohol recovery, AIDS education; and arts projects and festivals.

Locations: VFP has myriad locations, including the war-torn countries of the world, within its network.

Supervision: Moderate to high. Each program has about twelve volunteers to a group and a host or program coordinator.

Costs: The participant pays $200 for room, board, and registration for the two- or three-week workcamp. This is a flat rate for anywhere in the world. College credit is also available for an additional $300 to $500, but it has to be coordinated in advance. See the Web site for details.

WorldTeach
www.worldteach.org
E-mail: info@worldteach.org
c/o Center for International Development
Harvard University
79 John F. Kennedy Street
Cambridge, MA 02138
Phone: 617-495-5527
Toll-free: 1-800-4-TEACH-0

Description: "WorldTeach is a nonprofit, nongovernmental organization based at the Center for International Development at Harvard that provides opportunities for individuals to make a meaningful contribution to international education by living and working as volunteer teachers in developing countries."

WorldTeach offers volunteer opportunities that range in time from a summer to an entire year. Many of the host countries offer financial assistance, while others offer to pay the entire program cost for the participant. Expect to start out teaching English, with options to pursue other areas. The Honduras program, for instance, offers training for nature guides.

Locations: Chile, China, Costa Rica, Ecuador, Honduras, Marshall Islands, Namibia, and Poland.

Supervision: Low. The participant will be expected to act as a respected adult of the community.

Costs: The Marshall Islands program is fully funded by that government, while China's costs $1,000 for the entire year. Other yearlong programs require fees above $4,000. The Web site has great fund-raising tips for participants and includes information about filing federal income taxes on any money earned abroad through this program.

World-Wide Opportunities on Organic Farms
www.wwoof.org
P.O. Box 2675
Lewes BN7 1RB
United Kingdom

Description: "The organization's mission is to give you first-hand experience of organic or other ecologically sound growing methods. . . . To give you experience of life in the countryside. . . . To help the organic movement, which is labor-intensive and does not rely on artificial fertilizers, herbicides, or pesticides. . . . To give people a chance to meet, talk, learn, and exchange views with others in the organic movement. . . . To provide you with an opportunity to learn about life in the host country by living and working together."

A service organization that connects willing workers with organic farms throughout the world. What is expected? "The help you give your host will be variable, including sowing, making compost, gardening, planting, cutting wood, weeding, making mud bricks, harvesting, fencing, building, typing, packing, milking, or feeding. The help you give is an arrangement made between you and your host. The volunteering involved should not be exploitative of either the volunteer or the host. Often hosts themselves work long hours seven days a week and may expect you to do likewise. WWOOF suggests a fair exchange is six hours of solid help per day, six days per week, with a full day off each week to relax and explore the area." Each country in the WWOOF network has a book listing its organic farms that can be purchased through the WWOOF Web site.

Locations: Australia, Austria, Canada, the Czech Republic, Denmark, Finland, Germany, Ghana, Hawaii, Italy, Japan, Korea, Nepal, New Zealand, Slovenia, Sweden, Switzerland, Togo, and Uganda.

Supervision: Low to moderate. Usually the WWOOF host will serve as a pseudo-chaperone for the volunteer, but is not directly responsible for him or her.

Costs: An inexpensive way to travel to many interesting places of the world. Each country in the network has a different price for the book listing of farms, but most are very reasonable, and costs from farm to farm depend on personal arrangements that the volunteer makes with the host.

Studying—United States

Studying in the United States presents a wide range of possibilities, from learning in a traditional classroom setting to going off on an educational adventure in the wilderness. The advantages of such study include developing or supplementing an academic area or skill, connecting learning to the real world, exploring a new area or region of the United States, and even having an opportunity to earn college credit.

National Outdoor Leadership School
www.nols.edu
E-mail: admissions@nols.edu
284 Lincoln Street
Lander, WY 82520-2848
Phone: 307-332-5300
Toll-free: 1-800-710-NOLS

Description: "When NOLS students step into the world's wild places, they carry not only their backpacks, but also the weight of forty years of experience in expeditioning." Since 1965, the National Outdoor Leadership School has provided structured outdoor education opportunities for participants. Its curricula are designed around leading small groups in the wilderness, but the "lessons transfer to your life when you participate in groups at school, in sports, and at work." College credit generally is available. Open to all ages. Those under eighteen years of age require a parent's or guardian's consent to apply.

The core idea is the extended expedition, one of sufficient length that a person can learn and practice the skills over and over again. That is the backbone of every NOLS course, and today the school is widely recognized as a leader in the extended expedition, from two weeks to twelve.

Locations: Courses are offered primarily in the western United States, but also in Asia, Australia, and New Zealand.

Supervision: High. Groups travel with a teacher who accompanies participants throughout the course.

Costs: There is an application fee. Tuition and equipment deposits vary according to location and type of course, but expect to pay at least $4,000 for a thirty-day course. Financial aid (including scholarships from $500 to $1,500) is available for applicants "who show great potential to excel as NOLS students and who would be unable to attend without financial aid." NOLS courses are accepted for academic credit in many colleges and universities. The Web site shows comparison of the costs of taking NOLS courses for one semester versus attending a state university for a semester.

New York Film Academy
www.nyfa.com
E-mail: film@nyfa.com

100 East Seventeenth Street
New York, NY 10003
Phone: 212-674-4300

Description: The New York Film Academy is designed for students who are interested in the film industry. Students can take classes in acting, filmmaking, screenplay writing, 3D animation, and sound. The school offers many short workshops that usually last four to six weeks and also has a yearlong filmmaking program. Students get to make four of their own movies during the one-year program. Look at the Web site alumni to get an idea of student projects after graduation.

Locations: California (Hollywood), Florida (Disney/MGM), New York, Florence, London, Paris, Harvard University, and Princeton University.

Supervision: Low. The workshops are classes that do not provide accommodation or real safekeeping while there. NYFA does, however, help participants find housing, if needed, but apply early.

Costs: Costs vary widely due to the amount of time spent, but expect to pay around $6,000 for an eight-week course and $12,500 for the year. Participants can apply for career-training loans, but no scholarships or grants are available to offset program costs.

Sea Education Association
www.sea.edu
P.O. Box 6
Woods Hole, MA 02543
Phone: 508-540-3954
Toll-free: 1-800-552-3633

Description: SEA's mission is to be established at the leading edge of undergraduate education in the marine sciences. It provides programs "whose magic lies in the combination of knowledge gleaned in the classroom and its application at sea." SEA offers full-credit programs that are conducted at its campus in Woods Hole, MA. Students do course work in oceanography, nautical science, and maritime studies for the first half of the program on campus, followed by hands-on sailing, training, and research projects onboard tall ships. Credit is transferable to most colleges.

Locations: Woods Hole, MA.

Supervision: High. Students will have educators with them on their trips.

Costs: Fees are equivalent to college costs and cover tuition, room, and board as well as lab and book fees. Courses start at around $3,000 for six weeks. "SEA's undergraduate programs are designed to be a regular part of an undergraduate curriculum. After successfully completing the program, you receive the equivalent of a full semester's academic credit."

Tom Brown, Jr.'s Tracker School
www.trackerschool.com
E-mail: info@trackerschool.com
P.O. Box 173
92 Valley Station Road
Asbury, NJ 08802
Phone: 908-479-4681

Description: A school that teaches the Native American way of survival to all of its students. Based on the teachings of an Apache Scout named Stalking Wolf, the Tracker School is run by Tom Brown, one of the most experienced outdoorsmen in the United States. Be prepared to look at your life and the environment in a completely different light. The Tracker School also offers around thirty courses in various subjects that aren't necessarily survival-related, such as its acclaimed and highly popular philosophy course.

Locations: Classes are offered in California, Florida, and New Jersey, depending on the time of year.

Supervision: High. Students will be with well-trained instructors the length of the class.

Costs: Each weeklong class costs $900 in Florida and $950 in New Jersey.

Studying—International

Each year more than 160,000 American students study abroad, many through programs or arrangements with their home college or university. Advantages include interacting with students from a variety of countries; learning about different education and learning cultures; developing fluency in a language or culture; and, in many cases, having the option to gain college credit. Applications can be routine or rigorous, depending on the program or institution, and costs can range from modest to the equivalent of a year at a private college or university in the United States.

As with the domestic education options, studying abroad can be classroom based or centered on a learning adventure in the mountains or wilderness or even on the high seas.

ACCENT International
www.accentintl.com
E-mail: info@accentintl.com

870 Market Street, Suite 1026
San Francisco, CA 94102
Toll-free: 1-800-869-9291

Description: "ACCENT is an international education organization that works with more than fifty American colleges and
universities to provide high-quality study-abroad programs.
While some ACCENT programs require students to be currently enrolled in a college or university, others are open to students and nonstudents alike. ACCENT students earn
transferable college credit from the institution sponsoring the
program, while attending courses that incorporate the local culture with on-site lectures at museums, monuments, and historical sites."
Locations: ACCENT offers courses in Florence, London,
Madrid, Paris, and Rome.
Supervision: Low. A study-abroad program that gives a high degree of freedom to students.
Costs: Costs vary widely. A two-month program in Madrid costs
$5,300 in an apartment or $6,200 with a homestay; Paris costs
$6,300 for a three-month program, not including a homestay. See
individual programs for a detailed list of what the price includes.
Airfare is never included.

AmeriSpan (see pages 138–139 for full description)

British American Educational Foundation
www.baef.org
E-mail: scholars@baef.org
P.O. Box 33
Larchmont, NY 10538
Phone: 914-834-2064

Description: Since 1966, the British American Educational Foundation has provided opportunities for American students to study at British boarding schools. BAEF works with students and their families to find and get admitted to appropriate schools and provides ongoing support throughout a student's time abroad. BAEF has a special focus on students between high school and college.

Locations: Many schools throughout England.

Supervision: Moderate to high. Supervision is like what your student would have at a college in the United States.

Costs: Depending on the exchange rate, "an English school costs about the same as an American boarding school" or college. Airfare is not included. There is an application fee, an evaluation and school placement fee, and an additional fee to help cover support services. Scholarships sometimes are available. According to the site, costs are around $12,000 a semester.

CESA Languages Abroad
www.cesalanguages.com
E-mail: info@cesalanguages.com
CESA House
Pennance Road
Lanner, Cornwall TR16 5TQ
United Kingdom
Phone: 011-44-120-921-1800 from U.S.

Description: If a main goal of the gap year is learning a new language and being able to use it well, CESA is an ideal program. CESA language schools are intense language immersion and classroom programs that can run for two weeks or more. CESA accepts beginners and more advanced students, although beginners have fewer choices for start dates, so check out the dates early. See the Gap Year section on the Web site for information specific to time-off options, including language immersion programs that run from eight to twenty weeks.

Locations: Costa Rica, Ecuador, France, Germany, Greece, Italy, Japan, Mexico, Morocco, Portugal, Russia, and Spain.

Supervision: Moderate. Since there are twenty-five classes a week, much of the student's time is spent in the classroom, but on the weekends the students are free to do as they wish.

Costs: A twelve-week course generally costs around $1,700, but keep in mind that accommodation, daily living, and travel costs may not be included in these fees. College credit is offered for these language programs.

Costa Rica Language School
www.costaricalanguageschool.com
E-mail: costaricalanguageschool@yahoo.com
669-8000 Ministerios
Casa del Banquete
Pérez Zeledón, San José
Costa Rica
Phone: 011-506-369-8857

Description: Set in two locations in Costa Rica, CRLS offers a personalized language immersion experience. Students can choose from a standard or deluxe program, depending on how much attention they would like and how much Spanish they want to learn. Students (in the standard class) will have classes every day, with one surfing lesson a week, and will also have the chance to discover the culture and people of this incredible country. The deluxe program gives the opportunity to take dancing, cooking, surfing, and language courses, not to mention a homestay. This program is run by Costa Ricans, which gives participants a *Tico* feel, rather than being just another tourist.

Locations: San Isidro (a small city in Costa Rica's central valley) and Dominical (one of the best surfing beaches in the world).

Supervision: Moderate to high. All tours are supervised by native Costa Ricans and the host family.

Costs: Four weeks of the standard class cost $1,000, while the deluxe class will run $1,200 for the same length of time. Contact CRLS for more details on pricing of stays beyond four weeks.

Council on International Educational Exchange

www.ciee.org
7 Custom House Street, 3rd Floor
Portland, ME 04101
Phone: 207-553-7600
Toll-free: 1-800-40-STUDY

Description: Since 1947, the Council on International Educational Exchange has offered study abroad opportunities around the world. CIEE's mission is to "help people gain understanding, acquire knowledge, and develop the skills needed to live in a globally interdependent and culturally diverse world." CIEE Study Centers provide curricula "specifically designed with the American undergraduate in mind" and support students through specialized services and activities. Students must be affiliated with a college or university. "CIEE is a leader in security and safety for students studying abroad and continues to be committed to the operation of safe, secure, study experiences." See the Web site for useful information on safety and health concerns for studying abroad.

Locations: More than thirty countries in Africa, Asia, Australia, Europe, Latin America, and the Middle East.

Supervision: Varied. Programs exist for working abroad and studying abroad, and the supervision level changes with the program.

CIEE provides a twenty-four-hour emergency toll-free number and contacts in every region overseas, including those responsible for emergency preparedness plans.

Costs: Program fees are equivalent to tuition at a private college. Some scholarships and travel grants are available. All program participants are covered by accident and sickness insurance.

The Experiment in International Living
www.usexperiment.org
E-mail: eil@worldlearning.org
Kipling Road, P.O. Box 676
Brattleboro, Vermont 05302-0676
Toll-free: 1-800-345-2929

Description: EIL's mission is to foster peace through understanding, communication, and cooperation. It offers programs for high school students that involves living with a host family as well as having an area concentration. The student may choose community service, language studies, eco-adventure, travel, arts, or peace and conflict studies. The programs run during the summer and usually last for about a month. EIL prides itself on the diversity of its program participants and boasts of students from twenty-two different countries among its 2003 groups. Some programs have a one-year foreign language prerequisite. See the Web site for a program matrix that lists locations, costs, and other relevant information.

Locations: Destinations throughout Africa, Asia, Europe, Latin America, and South America.

Supervision: High. A group leader accompanies the group and takes care of logistics and travel arrangements.

Costs: Programs average four weeks in length and costs range from $4,500 to $5,500 and include international transportation.

Flying Fish
www.flyingfishonline.com
25 Union Road
Cowes, Isle of Wight PO31 7TW
United Kingdom
Phone: 011-44-198-328-0641 from U.S.

Description: Flying Fish offers many water sports courses including sailing, diving, windsurfing, and surfing in many areas of the world. For a gap year, one can earn their divemaster certification, become a yachtmaster, or become a certified instructor in surfing, windsurfing, or diving. The company also offers shorter programs for winter sports. According to the Web site's gap-year section, "Major American universities officially back the idea of a gap year before enrolling, and the number of U.S. students on Flying Fish programs grows each year." Check out the Consumer Info section as well to see Flying Fish's affiliations as a measure of financial assurance.
Locations: Australia, Canada, Cyprus, Egypt, Greece, and the United Kingdom,
Supervision: Varies, depending on location.
Costs: Vary widely.

The Institute for Central American Development Studies
www.icads.org
E-mail: info@icads.org
Dept. 826
P.O. Box 025216
Miami, FL 33102-5216
Phone: 011-506-225-0508 from U.S.

Description: ICADS is dedicated to filling "the information gap in foreign policy between North American citizens and their governments, promoting a deeper understanding of the Central American region."

With placements in Costa Rica and Nicaragua, ICADS is a study-abroad program that offers courses in Spanish and two semester-length programs—a field course in sustainable development and resource management and an internship and research program. Each is meant to educate students in the problems facing Central American sustainable development.

Locations: Costa Rica and Nicaragua.

Supervision: Moderate. Students will be in a school for much of their time with ICADS, so supervision will be relatively high, but during internships students will be given freedom, with support as needed.

Costs: A semester-long program that offers fifteen hours of academic credit will cost participants about $7,900. For an additional fee of $200, transfer of credits can be arranged through Hampshire College in the United States. According to the Web site, other American colleges accept credits directly.

The International Partnership for Service-Learning and Leadership (see pages 150–151 for full description)

ITHAKA
www.ithakasemester.org
E-mail: info@ITHAKAsemester.org
5500 Prytania Street, No. 102
New Orleans, LA 70115
Phone: 504-269-2303

Description: ITHAKA offers a "rigorous experiential and academic work-study immersion in Greek culture." Courses cover areas such as language, culture, poetry, writing, mythology, and current affairs. ITHAKA is modeled after a Greek family or a *parea,* a community of friends bound together by common purpose, common laws, loyalty, and affection. Having forged its own learning community, ITHAKA is integrated into the Greek community at large. Schedules are flexible to allow for participation in local and community events and group work projects. ITHAKA is designed for students between high school and college or students who are in college.

Locations: Greece.

Supervision: Contact program for details.

Costs: Fees (covering tuition, room and board, and field trips) are equivalent to college tuition and may change based on exchange rates and other factors. Travel and books are not included. Some financial aid is available.

LEAPNow (Lifelong Education Alternatives and Programs)

www.leapnow.org
E-mail: info@leapnow.org
P.O. Box 1817
Sebastopol, CA 95473
Phone: 707-431-7265

Description: "This nine-month program includes a three-month semester of language, service, and cultural immersion in Central America or Asia and a twelve-week individual internship. Also included are career and job-readiness counseling, a curriculum of life skills learning and a 'formal rite of passage' that also involves the parents." The program is designed to replace the first year of college or fill a gap year between high school and college. A six-month program also is available.

Locations: Asia, Central America, and the South Pacific.
Supervision: High. Group leaders accompany participants.
Costs: Fees are equivalent to college tuition and include all programs and activities, food and lodging, one year of college credit, and two round-trip international airfares. The leap year costs approximately $24,000.

Nacel Open Door
www.nacelopendoor.org
E-mail: info@nacelopendoor.org
1536 Hewitt Avenue, Box 268
St. Paul, MN 55104
Toll-free: 1-800-622-3553

Description: Nacel helps today's youth learn to understand and appreciate the world's cultural and linguistic diversity. Nacel believes that young people "benefit from experiences that complement their classroom learning, help them develop an awareness of their role as world citizens, and instill in them an ability to enjoy and adapt to diversity and change." It also believes that "opportunities to participate in such experiences must be accessible and affordable to as wide a range of people as possible."

Nacel is a study-abroad program for younger people fifteen to eighteen years old. The program offers homestays that involve attending schools with host brothers and sisters for either a semester of the American school year or summer.
Locations: Argentina, Australia, Brazil, France, Germany, Ireland, Japan, Mexico, New Zealand, Quebec, Spain, and Uruguay.
Supervision: Moderate. Nacel has in-country and local coordinators in each host country in addition to offices in the United States for support purposes.

Costs: Nacel includes international airfare and medical insurance in the fee, which averages about $5,500 for a semester, depending on airfare to the destination.

Semester At Sea
www.semesteratsea.com
E-mail: info@semesteratsea.com
Institute for Shipboard Education
811 William Pitt Union
Pittsburgh, PA 15260
Phone: 412-648-7490
Toll-free: 1-800-854-0195

Description: Semester At Sea provides a study-abroad program that offers students the chance to travel around the world on a veritable cruise ship. The boat circles the globe, stopping at select port cities for about five days at a time in order for students to see the cultural and ecological differences of each area. At each port city the students are offered choices among field study programs that can include homestays, museum visits, and mountain hikes. Students can choose from a variety of courses offered to find the ones that best match their field of study. The journey lasts for three months and a week.
Locations: The port cities may change from program to program. Sample sites include Brazil, Cambodia, Canada, Cuba, Hong Kong, India, Japan, South Africa, Tanzania, Thailand, and Vietnam.
Supervision: Low to moderate. Since this is a study-abroad program, students will be expected to act like mature adults, but will have the same supervision infrastructure as a university would have.
Costs: The cabin rates for a double or triple cabin that includes

tuition, room, and board is $14,975 per person. Financial aid from home institutions can be used to defray costs, and college credit for courses is awarded through the University of Pittsburgh, credits which (according to the Web site) are "readily transferable."

The WorldSmart Leadership Program
www.upwithpeople.org
E-mail: apply@worldsmart.org
Up with People, Inc.
1675 Broadway, Suite 1460
Denver, CO 80202
Toll-free: 1-877-264-8856

Description: The WorldSmart Leadership Program is designed to build understanding among nations and to spark people to action in meeting the needs of their communities, countries, and the world; and to equip young people with the leadership qualities of global perspective, integrity, and motivation to service.

This is a semester-long, study-abroad program for youth and is affiliated with Up with People. Students begin the program with an orientation in Denver, Colorado, and then travel to eighteen communities on different continents with a team of educators. They generally stay with host families. The Web site includes a section for parents that provides program information on costs and safety. Participants are between the ages of eighteen and twenty-nine.

Locations: Destination cities vary.

Supervision: Moderate to high. Participants are with leaders when traveling as a group, but during homestays supervision is relatively low.

Costs: The program costs $14,500 and includes tuition, travel, housing, and meals. Approximately $400,000 in needbased scholarships is awarded each year. College credit is awarded for course work through the University of Colorado at Denver.

Youth for Understanding
www.yfu-usa.org
Email: admissions@yfu.org
6400 Goldsboro Road, Suite 100
Bethesda, MD 20817
Toll-free: 1-866-4-YFU-USA

Description: Youth for Understanding is an international exchange and educational organization that offers more than a hundred programs in thirty countries for high school students and recent high school graduates. The organization works to "commit ourselves to finding new and innovative ways to inspire and engage a growing base of participants inclusive of racial, ethnic, and geographic diversity and increasingly open to all regardless of socioeconomic status." Participants live with a host family and learn a new language and culture during an academic year, academic semester, or summer program. Students from age fifteen to nineteen may enroll for semester or year-long programs.
Locations: Global graduate programs in Denmark, Hungary, and the Ukraine; academic programs in Germany, Latvia, Norway, Russia, Spain, Sweden, and Venezuela.
Supervision: Moderate. Homestays are common in the countries.
Costs: The yearlong programs cost about $7,000. Fees vary according to country and program specifics.

||||||||||||||||||||||||||||||||||||||||||||||||||

Exploring and
Traveling—United States

Students can hike, bike, travel, or explore as a segment of a gap-year experience. In the process, they can take advantage of the natural resources and diverse regions (from urban to rural) of the United States.

National Park Service
www.nps.gov
Contact through the Web site.

Description: The national parks of the United States are well-maintained recreational areas available for public use. National parks can be found everywhere in the states, some larger and more popular than others. The Appalachian Trail, for instance, winds through the national parks of the eastern seaboard from Georgia to Maine. Search the database of parks and trails on the

NPS Web site. Make sure you get the proper permits to hike and camp within national park grounds.

Locations: Everywhere in the United States.

Costs: Most national parks have small fees for parking or permits, but don't expect to pay much relative to other exploring options.

Outward Bound
www.outwardbound.com
E-mail: info@obusa.com
100 Mystery Point Road
Garrison, NY 10524
Toll-free: 1-866-467-7651

Description: Outward Bound's mission is "to conduct safe, adventure-based programs structured to inspire self-esteem, self-reliance, concern for others, and care for the environment." Outward Bound expeditions are not for the faint of heart! The organization has been around for sixty years and has provided high-quality and safe adventures since its commencement. Outward Bound sessions vary in length from nine to fifty-five days and involve such adventures as kayaking, backpacking, climbing, and a solitary day in the wilderness. OB expeditions are known for their positive impact on participants in areas such as teamwork, self-confidence, and appreciation of nature.

Outward Bound continues to excel in its long-standing tradition of using the wilderness as a "classroom" for self-discovery. However, its influence goes far beyond the individuals who participate in the wilderness courses. The programs touch the lives of more people than ever before, today reaching more than 60,000 people each year.

The four wilderness schools (Outward Bound West, Hurricane Island, Voyageur, and North Carolina), the two independent urban centers (New York City Outward Bound Center and Thompson Island Outward Bound Education Center), and the primary and secondary school-reform program (Expeditionary Learning Outward Bound) are each governed by a separate board of trustees, and they are bound together as a federation. The schools and centers adhere to the essential Outward Bound curriculum and the national safety policies. Outward Bound USA, based in Garrison, NY, is responsible for chartering the schools and centers, ensuring the safety and the quality of all programs, providing leadership, expanding scholarship resources, and developing the Outward Bound movement in the United States. Through each of these Outward Bound organizations and through the various programs, students develop self-reliance, responsibility, teamwork, confidence, compassion, and environmental and community stewardship in all of the Outward Bound programs and courses.

Locations: Sites are located across the Americas and in Europe, as well as the Bahamas.

Supervision: High. Outward Bound instructors accompany each group of participants and are highly qualified in outdoor and group leadership skills.

Costs: A fifty-five-day course costs about $5,500. Shorter programs are priced from about $1,200. Scholarship aid is available.

Trailplace
www.trailplace.com
Center for Appalachian Trail Studies
1800 Brandy Woods Trail, SE
Conyers, GA 30013
Phone: 770-679-0633

Description: If you are willing to test your limits and hike the 2,174 miles of the Appalachian Trail, to Maine all the way from Georgia, start your journey here. This Web site offers used hiking and camping equipment for sale, tips for hikers, breakdowns of the sections of trail, and a photo gallery of trails. The site also features contact information for experienced hikers who know the trails.

Costs: Free.

Exploring and Traveling—International

Through global exploration and travel, students can see the world while testing their travel and communications skills, learning about other cultures and languages, and meeting interesting people along the way.

BSES Expeditions
www.bses.org.uk
E-mail: bses@rgs.org
At the Royal Geographical Society
1, Kensington Gore
London SW7 2AR
Phone: 011-44-207-591-3141 from U.S.

Description: BSES offers adventurous expeditions through many extremely rugged parts of the world. The gap-year expeditions are three months long and involve a research project in one of four areas (in the South African program): game conservation, game management, rock art study, and historical study of the AmaZulu. There are also many shorter expeditions, usually lasting around four weeks, offered all over the world.

Locations: Gap-year programs are offered only in South Africa and Chile at this time, but shorter four-week expeditions are offered in thirty-two wilderness areas, including Alaska, British Columbia, Greenland, Kenya, Montana, Peru, South Georgia, and Sweden,

Supervision: High. An expedition leader accompanies the group, as does a doctor. See the Safety Policy section on the Web site.

Costs: Expect to pay $5,500 for the gap-year programs; four-week programs start at about $3,300.

Earthwatch Institute
www.earthwatch.org
E-mail: info@earthwatch.org.uk
3 Clock Tower Place, Suite 100
Box 75
Maynard, MA 01754
Toll-free: 1-800-776-0188

Description: Earthwatch Institute takes groups on expeditions as volunteer researchers in remote regions of the world that are in need of sustainable solutions. Its expeditions have many different fields of study, including archaeology, biodiversity, conservation research initiatives, cultural diversity, endangered ecosystems, global exchange, oceanography, scuba diving, and world health. Volunteers will help fund the operating costs and will work for ten days on a project.

Locations: Any region of the world that could be desired. Check the Web site for details.

Supervision: High. Each project has a leader, and participants work directly with that leader for the length of the stay.

Costs: Expect to pay at least $1,000 for a weeklong expedition, with expeditions in more exotic places being more costly. Fees may be tax deductible, according to the Web site.

Madventurer (see pages 152–153 for full description)

Working and Interning—United States

Earning money during segments of a gap year is an obvious and even necessary choice for many students. With enough planning, students can have the opportunity to work or intern in a position that complements their educational interests, allows them to "try out" a career and get a sense of what responsibility and accountability entail in the "real world," helps build a résumé, and establishes professional contacts.

In addition to the resources below, comprehensive books and guides to internships and job leads are available through the Internet or at your local bookstore. Students can also network to uncover opportunities, create their own internships through researching an organization and "making the case" why their services are needed, or even become an entrepreneur!

DATABASES AND LISTINGS OF INTERNSHIPS AND JOBS

JobMonkey
www.jobmonkey.com
E-mail: JMHelp2@JobMonkey.com
P.O. Box 3956
Seattle, WA 98124
Toll-free: 1-877-258-7519

Description: This Web-based job database includes work in a wide variety of fields—in the airline industry, theme parks, guides on buses or outdoors, teaching English, cruise ships, ski resorts, and casinos. JobMonkey's stated mission is to help employment seekers "find seasonal or year-round jobs working for employers who can offer unique opportunities to travel the world, have fun, and earn money doing it." The site also offers tips on careers and working and traveling.
Costs: Free.

Monster
www.monster.com

Description: A job database with thousands of job listings for someone looking for a career or in search of summer work. Monster also offers tips on how to get the job of your dreams through résumé-writing guides as well as a networking service that "helps you meet the right people."
Costs: Free to check out listings and/or to upload résumé or profile.

Politixgroup
www.politixgroup.com

Description: This Web site provides information and links to internships in Washington, DC, including those at the White House or U.S. Congress and with political parties, government agencies, think tanks, and policy organizations. Most internships require affiliation with a college or university.
Costs: Free to check out listings.

Rising Star Internships
www.rsinternships.com

Description: This site provides information on and links to internships in a variety of areas—from international business to golf and tennis.
Costs: Free to check out listings.

Young Politicians of America
www.ypa.org
P.O. Box 5286
Walnut Creek, CA 94596-1286
Toll-free: 1-800-616-2516

Description: The Young Politicians of America was founded to "expand the democratic experience to the youth of our society." Through YPA chapters, young people volunteer, discuss, and encourage each other to understand government's role. The Web site includes links to hundreds of internships in a variety of organizations—government, nonprofit, media, and academic and service organizations. Many are open to high school students and high school graduates. There is no eligibility requirement or fee for access to internship listings.
Costs: Free to check out listings.

Youth Service America
www.ysa.org

Description: Youth Service America is a resource center that partners with organizations committed to "increasing the quality and quantity of volunteer opportunities for young people in America." Listings include national and international internships and job opportunities.
Costs: Free to check out listings.

PROGRAMS

Dynamy Internship Year
www.dynamy.org
E-mail: info-email@dynamy.org
27 Sever Street
Worcester, MA 01609
Phone: 508-755-2571

Description: A year-long program that includes three full-time, nine-week internships; an Outward Bound course; community involvement; educational seminars for college credit; and weekly advising. Students seventeen to twenty-two years of age are invited to apply for several dozen openings.
Locations: Worcester, Massachusetts, and throughout the United States for internships and Outward Bound.
Supervision: High. The weekly advising and ongoing support make this a well-supervised endeavor.
Costs: Tuition for an internship is equivalent to college tuition, with additional fees for housing. The year will cost about $13,000,

while a semester costs $7,100. College credit is awarded for seminars through Clark University.

Environmental Careers Organization
www.eco.org
30 Winter Street
Boston, MA 02108
Phone: 617-426-4375

Description: ECO's mission is to protect and enhance the environment through the development of diverse leaders, the promotion of careers, and the inspiration of individual action. ECO accomplishes this through internships, career advice, career tools, research, and consulting.

It helps place students and graduates looking to get a career started in the environmental field in internships with one of many reputable conservation and environmental employers. Examples of internships include park rangers, wildlife biologists, EPA law associates, archaeological aides or technicians, and work as a plant ecologist.

ECO is mostly for college graduates, but an interested student without much college experience may still contact ECO for opportunities. Some programs require "educational background" in certain areas rather than a degree.

Group Workcamps Foundation
www.groupworkcamps.com
E-mail: info@groupworkcamps.com
P.O. Box 599
1515 Cascade Avenue
Loveland, CO 80539-0599
Toll-free: 1-800-774-3838

Description: Founded in 1977, Group Workcamps Foundation camps offer the "premier summer missions experience for church youth." The Web site describes group camps "as the ultimate expression of Christian service—group camps offer a fun, challenging, faith-building adventure youth leaders and their students will never forget."

A typical camp brings together approximately 400 students and adult leaders to provide more than 12,000 hours of free service to a community. Camp participants come from churches of many denominations across the country. In Workcamps, students participate in community service through completing basic home repairs and painting homes at no cost to the disabled, disadvantaged, or elderly. In the Week of Hope program, students contribute through working with local health and human service agencies or churches to provide personal assistance to individuals. In the Service Expedition initiative, students participate in community service abroad. The ages of student participants range from fourteen to twenty.

Group Workcamps hires staff to support the camps in more than sixty locations each summer. Summer staff crews travel in teams to different sites to set up the camp and help coordinate the week's activities. Summer staff then tear down the camp equipment and are invited to relax for a day or two before traveling on to the next destination. See the Web site for details on hiring eligibility and to apply online.

Locations: Sites include locations across the United States and in Belize, Canada, and Puerto Rico.

Supervision: Staff provides supervision and the Web site reports that the organization "takes this responsibility seriously." The Web site adds that "each service site is supervised by at least one adult, adults are assigned to sleep in classrooms with their youth groups, and participants are not allowed in the sleeping areas of the opposite sex."

Costs/Compensation: Compensation is approximately $3,000 for 12 weeks. In addition, meal and lodging expenses are covered and all travel is paid for except a trip to the organization's headquarters in Colorado at the beginning of the summer session (which the staff member covers).

NASCAR Diversity Internship Program

www.diversityinternships.com
E-mail: info@diversityinternships.com
NASCAR Diversity Department
1801 W. International Speedway Boulevard
Daytona Beach, FL 32114
Phone: 386-253-0611

Description: Through the NASCAR Diversity Internship Program, the National Association for Stock Car Auto Racing (NASCAR) offers ten-week, full-time, paid summer internships to college students who are of Alaskan Native, American Indian, Asian/Pacific Island, African American, Hispanic, or of other racial minority descent. The program is designed to introduce students "to the world of NASCAR and the exciting career opportunities available throughout the motorsports industry." Internships focus on areas such as broadcasting, communications, competition, design, engineering, event management, fund-raising, business, licensing, marketing, media services, public relations, sales, and sports marketing. Applicants must have a 3.0 grade point average (on a scale of 4.0).

NASCAR also offers internships for students of all cultural backgrounds. Information is available through the NASCAR

Jobline at (386) 947-6878 or the NASCAR employment Website at http://employment.nascar.com.

Locations: Internships are offered at locations across the United States (see Web site for specific sites and descriptions of internship opportunities).

Supervision: The work experience is structured and supervised; students are on their own when not at work.

Costs/Compensation: Compensation varies based on the position and location of the internship. Students may be provided with subsidized housing or help with finding housing at the location. If the specific internship does not provide housing assistance, the intern is responsible for finding housing. Transportation to and from work is the intern's responsibility. In addition to "competitive wages," interns may receive tickets to a NASCAR Nextel Cup Series race.

PGA Tour Internship Program
www.pgatour.com/info/company/internships
E-mail: mcooney@pgatourhq.com
100 PGA Tour Boulevard
Ponte Vedra Beach, FL 32082
Phone: 904-285-3700

Description: The PGA Tour—the nonprofit organization that organizes golf tournaments—offers an internship for college students to "introduce the business side of golf." Students must have completed their sophomore year in college and have a 2.6 grade point average (on a scale of 4.0). The ten to thirteen week internships focus on areas such as event management, communications and public relations, marketing and business development, golf course design and construction, and more. Most internships are offered during the summer, however, there also are some year-round opportunities (see Web site for specific locations and description of current offerings). Internships are "enhanced by activities and projects that will allow you to gain a full picture of how the PGA Tour and other golf organizations work together to support our players, charities, and events on the PGA Tour, Champions Tour, and the Nationwide Tour." The internship orientation begins with a reception with golf industry staff.

The PGA Tour also offers a similarly structured Diversity Internship Program designed for students of African American, Asian American and Pacific Islander, Native American, or Hispanic descent.

Locations: Sites vary. Many internships are located at PGA Tour tournament locales—Atlanta, GA; Dearborn, MI; Sonoma, CA; Akron, OH; Rye, NY; McLean, VA; and Savannah, GA. Internship opportunities also are available in Ponte Vedra Beach, PGA Tour headquarters.

Supervision: The work experience is structured and supervised; off-work supervision will depend on the housing arrangements that vary depending on location.

Compensation: Compensation varies based on location and specific responsibilities, however, the PGA Tour says it offers "competitive wages." Up to $500 in travel expenses is provided. Subsidized housing may be provided, depending on location.

United States Public Interest Research Group
www.uspirg.org
E-mail: uspirg@pirg.org
218 D Street, SE
Washington, DC 20003
Phone: 202-546-9707

Description: "U.S. PIRG is an advocate for the public interest. When consumers are cheated, or the environment is threatened, or the voices of ordinary citizens are drowned out by special interest lobbyists, U.S. PIRG speaks up and takes action. We uncover threats to public health and well-being and fight to end them, using the time-tested tools of investigative research, media exposés, grassroots organizing, advocacy, and litigation. U.S. PIRG's mission is to deliver persistent, result-oriented public interest activism that protects our environment, encourages a fair, sustainable economy, and fosters responsive, democratic government."

U.S. PIRG offers undergraduates currently attending a university as well as graduates internships that allow them to work to change public policy on one of many areas of the United States public policy agenda. U.S. PIRG is a good option for someone who wants to get involved in the politics of change.

Locations: The national PIRG is based in Washington, DC, and was founded by the PIRGs common throughout the states. Contact your state's PIRG or U.S. PIRG for info.

Supervision: Low. This will be an internship for someone with an already in-tune sense of responsibility.

Costs/Compensation: Internships are sometimes paid, but contact programs for in-depth details.

The Venture Consortium
www.theventureconsortium.org
E-mail: venture@brown.edu
Box 1838
Providence, RI 02912
Phone: 401-863-2324

Description: "The Venture Consortium, a group of selective, private, liberal arts colleges and universities, is dedicated to the development of innovative programs to complement the liberal arts curriculum. It is designed to offer enriching work opportunities for students who want to extend their education beyond the classroom. On-campus advisors help students think through the nuts and bolts of planning for a leave of absence. Finally, the Venture Web site provides resources for planning a leave and other ways for students to get the most out of their leave-taking experience."

Services include a searchable job database and related information and support that help students from affiliated colleges find opportunities that are usually paid.

Headquartered at Brown University, member colleges include Bates, Brown, Connecticut Wesleyan, Franklin and Marshall, Holy Cross, Sarah Lawrence, Swarthmore, Syracuse, and Vassar. *Locations:* In the United States. Specific location depends on the position.

Supervision: Jobs vary widely.

Costs/Compensation: Most positions are paid.

Working and
Interning—International

If your student is planning to work overseas, make sure to find out whether a work permit is needed and, if so, whether he or she can get it. In many cases, the answer will be no, which means that he or she won't be able to work legally abroad. More broadly, the answer depends on the country and the length of time the student wants to work overseas.

Transitions Abroad, an excellent resource for gap-year students (see full description on pages 198 to 199), explains that a major obstacle to working abroad is the law: "All countries require special permission for foreigners to either work or reside for long periods of time. Whereas short-term tourists sometimes do not need a visa and student visas are granted relatively easily, work permit visas are normally available only through application by an employer who has offered you a job. The employer must show that you have unique skills and abilities not possessed by local citizens.

"This is expensive and time-consuming to prove, so most employers, who are subject to heavy fines if they hire illegally, will not offer a job to a foreigner who does not possess a work permit. Work exchange programs are one of the few legal ways around this. Note: it is also possible to work illegally, that is, without a work permit. Such jobs may turn up in restaurants and agriculture as well as in teaching English. [Transitions Abroad] cannot recommend working illegally because it puts you at risk of immediate deportation, possible fines, low wages (or no wages at all), and lack of legal protection or insurance in case of injury or illness."

Even with this caveat, there are organizations such as BUNAC (www.bunac.org) that will help individuals find jobs in select countries and will assist with work visas. However, they tend to be focused on setting you up and thereafter provide limited support.

Included below are programs that combine a short-term internship with travel, cultural exchange, or study and that may be valuable options for a time-off plan.

GENERAL RESOURCE

Transitions Abroad
www.transitionsabroad.com
P.O. Box 745
Bennington, VT 05201
Phone: 802-442-4827

Description: This "portal for work abroad, overseas travel, study abroad, and international living" is an excellent resource if you are looking into the option of taking time off. If you have any questions whatsoever, chances are this Web site can help answer them. Transitions Abroad is based on a magazine that features articles and resources on time-off options and study abroad. This site has high-quality links for time-off companies and work-abroad employment offerings. It also has tips on safety and countless travel tips that will save you time and money. Definitely one of the first places you should go when time off is on your mind. *Costs:* Free access to Web-based resources.

OTHER RESOURCES

AmeriSpan (see pages 138–139 for full description)

BUNAC
www.bunac.org
E-mail: info@bunacusa.org
P.O. Box 430
Southbury, CT 06488
Phone: 203-264-0901

Description: Each BUNAC program is designed to offer participants "a unique insight into a completely new culture and a chance to spend extended time working and traveling overseas." BUNAC helps participants secure jobs in eight countries. It provides an in-country orientation and accommodations for the first two nights. This organization has access to special visas that can help participants work for a long period of time, and it deals with the logistics of obtaining a work visa, making sure they get processed quickly.
Locations: Australia, Canada, England, Ireland, New Zealand, Scotland, South Africa, and the United States.

Supervision: Very low. After orientation, participants are on their own. BUNAC does have an in-country support staff, but independence is a big tenet of this program.
Costs: $475 for consulting services. (The cost of obtaining visas is included.)

English Language Teaching Assistant Program
www.eltap.org
Division of Education
University of Minnesota, Morris
Morris, MN 56267
Phone: 320-589-6400

Description: ELTAP offers a "low-cost international experience for future teachers that provides participants with the opportunity to work together, expand their ability to communicate with each other, and increase their understanding of each other's culture."

It features a small-scale study-abroad and continuing education program that facilitates internships in a number of countries for students who are studying education and are working toward a teaching certificate. Students are placed with host families and assist high school English teachers in their host country for four to eleven weeks.
Locations: Twenty-eight countries.
Supervision: An in-country coordinator verifies your work and oversees you in the classroom.
Costs: A flat rate of $3,063 is charged for the program. Those who complete the work receive twelve credits to satisfy their student teaching requirement.

Foundation for Sustainable Development
www.fsdinternational.org
E-mail: info@fsdinternational.org
870 Market Street, Suite 321
San Francisco, CA 94102
Phone: 415-283-4873

Description: FSD supports the efforts of grassroots development organizations in the developing world that are working to better their communities, environments, and the economic opportunities around them. Economic development begins with community development and is only sustainable if it comes from and is supported by the members of these communities.

FSD offers internships in the developing world for academic credit, short-term volunteer stints, and work-study courses. Internships are offered year-round for a minimum of eight weeks; work-study programs require touring a developing country while studying a topic such as international economic development, for three weeks or less.

Locations: Bolivia, Ecuador, Nicaragua, Peru, Tanzania, and Uganda.

Supervision: Varied. The work-study and short-term volunteer offerings have chaperones who look after participants and act as guides. The internship programs include a higher level of supervision, with an in-country coordinator visiting participants in their homestays for one or two days a week.

Costs: Highly structured programs like the ten-week summer internship cost about $2,400 (for Peru), while individual internships cost $1,600 for eight weeks and $300 more for each additional four weeks.

Go Abroad
www.goabroad.com

Description: The Web site of Go Abroad provides resources on international interning and working. It includes lists of work opportunities and information on travel, insurance, visas, and other issues.
Costs: Free.

Institute for Cultural Ecology
www.cultural-ecology.com
E-mail: info@cultural-ecology.com
P.O. Box 991
Hilo, HI 96721
Toll-free: 1-866-230-8508

Description: The Institute for Cultural Ecology was "founded on the conviction that visits to exotic destinations necessitate a commitment to cultural sensitivity and environmental stewardship."

ICE offers internships and field study programs in the Pacific region. Its programs usually have a concentration on environmental issues, but internships in other occupations are possible. The internships are available in environmental conservation, youth travel, museums, education, social advocacy, and information media.
Locations: Australia, Fiji, Hawaii, Nepal, New Zealand, and Thailand.
Supervision: Moderate to high. Interns work with small organizations within the host country and are looked after by the staff of those organizations rather than by ICE.
Costs: A twelve-week internship costs around $3,850 (not including airfare or food).

InterExchange
www.interexchange.org
E-mail: info@interexchange.org
161 Sixth Avenue
New York, NY 10013
Phone: 212-924-0446

Description: InterExchange was established thirty years ago with a mission "to promote cultural awareness, knowledge, and global competence among people from around the world through international exchange programs, offering work and training opportunities in the United States and abroad." The Web site includes information on jobs for students (for example, au pair and camp counselor positions) and on government regulations applicable to overseas employment.
Locations: Australia, Belgium, Costa Rica, France, Germany, Great Britain, the Netherlands, Norway, Peru, South Africa, and Spain.
Costs: Depends on program.

International Cooperative Education
www.icemenlo.com
E-mail: icemenlo@aol.com
15 Spiros Way
Menlo Park, CA 94025
Phone: 650-323-4944

Description: ICE's mission is to provide "American college and university students a unique opportunity to gain practical work experience abroad." It is designed for college students seeking to work abroad for an extended period of time. This organization will help set up job opportunities and work visas. This program is

similar to BUNAC USA, and we recommend comparing the two.
Locations: Argentina, Belgium, Bolivia, Chile, China, England, Germany, Japan, Peru, Singapore, Switzerland, Uruguay, and Vietnam.
Supervision: Low. This program is designed for responsible, mature applicants.
Costs: $1,000 for consulting services; paid internships.

JobMonkey (see 187 for full description)

Travellers Worldwide
www.travellersworldwide.com
E-mail: info@travellersworldwide.com
7 Mulberry-Close
Ferring, West-Sussex, BN12 5HY
United Kingdom
Phone: 011-44-190-370-0478

Description: Travellers Worldwide was founded to provide the opportunity for people from all over the world to experience what it is like to live and work in foreign countries and cultures. TW uses the fees from volunteers toward donations and much needed resources for communities in need. TW has programs in conservation, teaching English, cultural study, language study, and work placements. Participants can choose more than one of these options in more than one country.
Locations: Argentina, Brazil, Brunei, China, Cuba, Ghana, Guatemala, India, Kenya, Malaysia, Nepal, Russia, South Africa, Sri Lanka, the Ukraine, and Vietnam.
Supervision: Moderate. Travellers Worldwide operates through local organizations at each destination, each of which has a

leader who will pick the student up at the airport and occasionally check in throughout the program.

Costs: Three-month programs run about $2,700, with options to continue for as long as a year priced at lower rates. Check out their Web site for great fund-raising tips.

University of Michigan International Center
www.umich.edu/-icenter/overseas/work/waverweb.html

Description: The Web site of the University of Michigan's International Center includes a section on work abroad that features information on when and how to apply, visas, and costs, as well as short-term paid work, internships, volunteering, and teaching opportunities.

Costs: Free.

II. RESOURCES

Consultants and Counseling Services

In this section we provide information on resources that will be helpful in designing time-off experiences—consultants and counseling services, travel and housing, fund-raising, and health and safety.

The Center for Interim Programs, LLC
www.interimprograms.com
CONTACT INFORMATION, NEW JERSEY OFFICE
Holly Bull, President
195 Nassau Street, Suite 5
Princeton, NJ 08542
Phone: 609-683-4300
Fax: 609-683-4309
E-mail: hollybull@interimprograms.com

CONTACT INFORMATION, MASSACHUSETTS OFFICE
Joanna Lazarek, Vice President
P.O. Box 38-2347
Cambridge, MA 02238
Phone: 617-547-0980
Fax: 617-661-2864
E-mail: info@interimprograms.com

Description: The Center for Interim Programs was founded in 1980 and is the "first, and longest running, counseling service of its kind to be established in the United States." Interim has designed customized gap-year programs for thousands of individuals and is able to draw from more than 4,000 programs and other options.

Eligibility and Fees: Students fill out an application and are eligible for a free preliminary consultation by phone or in person. There is a flat fee of $1,900 for ongoing and personalized support, planning, guidance, and research for an individual's lifetime.

Taking Off
www.takingoff.net
CONTACT INFORMATION
Gail Reardon
12 Marlborough Street
Boston, MA 02116
Phone: 617-424-1606
Fax: 617-344-0481
E-mail: takingoff@takingoff.net

Description: Taking Off works with young people who are taking time away from the traditional classroom before, during, and after college and those who do not have higher education plans. Taking Off limits the number of clients they work with, so all clients have unlimited access to their staff and database. Taking Off provides a framework in which clients (in concert with their parents) create a safe, well-thought-out, and meaningful plan so as to ensure that "stopping out" does not become "dropping out." Taking Off believes that both the product (where a student goes and what they do) and the process are important. Their process teaches students how to figure out what they want, why they want it, and whether a given opportunity is a good fit with who they are and what they hope to do. The learning that takes place during this process goes beyond the plan for a gap year, continuing through a lifetime of choices and decisions.

Eligibility and Fees: Young people between the ages of seventeen and twenty-three. A "short-term consultation" for those students who have a focused area of interest is $900. Their flat fee, which provides unlimited consultation to clarify, craft, and implement a well-thought-out plan for the current time-off period and beyond, is $1,800.

Where You Headed

www.whereyouheaded.com
CONTACT INFORMATION
Robert P. Gilpin
P.O. Box 503
Milton, MA 02186
Phone: 617-698-8977
E-mail: info@whereyouheaded.com

Description: "Where You Headed is designed to serve students and their families who are looking for information and advice about the passage through high school and college—and all the twists and turns in between." Membership features include access to a searchable database of thousands of time-out opportunities, college admissions and transfer guidance, e-mail consultations with staff, links to resource and information sites, and more. Phone call consultations with staff also are available.

Eligibility and Fees: Services are designed for high school and college students. Options include a six-month membership for $80 and a twelve-month membership for $120. Students who qualify for an SAT fee waiver are offered free memberships.

Travel and Housing

Council on Standards for International Educational Travel
www.csiet.org
E-mail: mailbox@csiet.org
212 South Henry Street
Alexandria, VA 22314
Phone: 703-739-9050

Description: The Council on Standards for International Educational Travel (CSIET) is a nonprofit organization established to identify reputable international youth travel and exchange programs geared toward students of high school age. CSIET has established standards and publishes lists of organizations that meet the standards.
Costs: Free.

Hostelling International
www.hihostels.com
Hostelling International—USA
8401 Colesville Road, Suite 600
Silver Spring, MD 20910
Phone: 301-495-1240

Description: Hostelling International is the "leading provider of budget accommodation with 4,000 plus hostels in great locations around the world." Hostelling International—USA (www.hiusa.org) is a nonprofit membership organization founded in 1934 that runs 110 hostels in the United States that are inexpensive, safe, and clean. Students can identify and book hostels through the Web site.
Costs: A membership fee is required.

International Student Exchange ID Card
www.isecard.com

Description: The International Student Exchange ID Card is an internationally recognized ID and discount card available to students of any age and to youth between the ages of twelve and twenty-six. Cardholders receive discounts that range from 10 to 50 percent off for travel and at hotels, restaurants, shops, language schools, theaters, concerts, recreational facilities, and more. There are thousands of authorizing offices around the world. Check the Web site for specifics.
Costs: The card costs around $25 (a great bargain!).

Student Travel Agency
www.statravel.com

E-mail: enquiry@statravelgroup.com
Toll-free: 1-800-781-4040

Description: STA can play many different roles in a time-off experience. First and foremost is its ability to act as a travel agent for youths of the world by giving them discounts to many popular destinations. STA can offer discounts on some airfares as well as for thousands of hotels, train fare, restaurants, and gear. You must apply for an international student ID or international youth ID card to take advantage of all their services, but it is well worth it.

Locations: STA centers are all over the world, but STA is most easily accessible on the Internet or by phone.

Costs: The card costs only $22 and can save thousands on travel expenses.

Fund-Raising

An Internet search (key terms might include "gap year fund-raising" or "student fund-raising") will lead to myriad sites with ideas, examples, and other resources for find-raisers. Although a lot of information is geared toward gappers in the United Kingdom, most is also applicable to United States students. Rotary International and WorldTeach (see below) are two of the many sites and organizations that offer fund-raising information.

Rotary International
www.rotary.org

Rotary International has branches all over the world, and its Web site is a great resource for information about fund-raising and scholarships for time-off programs. Rotary sponsors kids that are going somewhere to make a difference in the world through volunteer work, or even a self-designed program. Contact your local Rotary Club to see what the options are.

WorldTeach
www.worldteach.org

WorldTeach has established a "proud history of contributing to international education and development and promoting cultural exchange through quality volunteer programs." The Web site includes good fund-raising tips and examples.

Health and Safety

The health and safety conditions overseas can vary day by day and from country to country. Here are some resources for checking on specifics.

- Center for Global Education (www.lmu.edu/globaled/index.html). The site resources include a "Student Study Abroad Safety Handbook," a Web-based handbook for American students on foreign laws and different cultures.
- Centers for Disease Control and Prevention's National Center for Infectious Diseases (www.cdc.gov/travel/index.htm). The Web site provides recommendations regarding immunizations, disease challenges, and other location-specific health information.
- Council on International Educational Exchange (www.ciee.org). The CIEE Web site has a useful section on "Health and Safety."

- Inter-Organization Task Force on Safety and Responsibility in Study Abroad (www.secussa.nafsa.org/safetyabroad). The Task Force was formed in 1997 by the Association of International Education Administrators (AIEA), the Section on U.S. Students Abroad (SECUSSA) of NAFSA: Association of International Educators, and the Council on International Educational Exchange (CIEE) to help "make study abroad as safe as possible."
- U.S. Department of State Tips for Students (http://travel.state.gov/studentinfo.html). This Web site provides information on medical insurance and what embassy and other offices can do to assist Americans who are abroad.
- U.S. Department of State Travel Warnings and Consular Information Sheets (http://travel.state.gov/travel/warnings_consular.html). This site provides updates on travel warnings regarding security, political instability, or health issues in countries and regions.

Acknowledgments

First and foremost, thank you to Adam Haigler for his exceptional writing, interviewing, and researching talents. This book is possible because of his inspiration, skills, humor, and patience.

Elisabeth Weed with Kneerim & Williams at Fish and Richardson is the world's best agent! Thank you for jump-starting this project, working on its behalf, and supporting it. Julie Mente at St. Martin's Press took on this work with uncommon professionalism and insight, providing advice and guidance along the way. Thanks to our copy editor, Donald J. Davidson, for his valuable suggestions, as well as to Kenneth J. Silver, the production editor who oversaw the making of this book. Julia Pastore was an early supporter who "made it happen," and Marian Lizzi helped mold the vision. In addition to his personal story, Matt Hendren lent researching and writing skills, expertise, time, and energy. Thank you as well to the North Carolina Writers' Network for allowing writers and editors to meet at their conference. (These opportunities can yield positive results!)

Kay Shaw Nelson has long set a professional standard for writers, and we have tried to emulate her in producing this book. Jennifer Minar, founder and managing editor of Writer's Break (www.writersbreak.com), is a steadfast supporter of writers, and we appreciate her encouragement.

Holly Bull, of the Center for Interim Programs, provided invaluable expertise and advice, and was always willing to take the time to listen to ideas and answer questions.

Other thank-yous go to the parents and colleagues who shared their time, observations, and words of wisdom. These include Wrenna Haigler, Sandy Buchanan, Pam Lassiter, Cary Milner, David Neidorf, Kathy Olson, Donna Rubin, Hal Shear, Bobbi and David Taylor, Grace and Larry Whatley, and Steve and Susan Widmar. Thank you to Jonathan Milner for continuing to inspire a future generation of leaders.

A special tribute is owed to the many students whose stories are noted in the book; their experiences and accomplishments are truly inspiring. They include Joseph Demille, Erika Dickson, Melea Glick, Matt Hendren, Will Hunt, Pippa King, Allison Lassiter, Mitchell Levene, David Miller, Jordan Price, David Roodhouse, Ben Rubin, Anya Shear, Dana Swanson, Scott Taylor, Laurel Wamsley, and Rusty Whatley.

Thanks as well to Jane Goldstone, of Global Routes, for her early understanding of our goals and for providing leads to extraordinary students and parents whom we were privileged to interview. Gail Reardon, of Taking Off; Bob Gilpin, of Where You Headed?; Betsy Hansel, of AFS International; and Peggy Chang, of the Venture Consortium, took the time to share insights based on their respective in-depth experience in the time-off field.

We are indebted to William F. Rowland, an authentic American hero, who has always told us to set our goals high.

Rachel Haigler, Rett Haigler, and Ashley Triplett contributed their support, patience, and humor throughout this project and command their own inspiring stories as they forge their intrepid pathways: We couldn't be prouder of you!

Last, but certainly not least, a thank-you to Isabel Haigler for her unfailing energy and enthusiasm. They sustained and inspired us during this project!

Program Index

Subject Index